Anne McDerm

The Ten Things Every Parent Needs to Know

A Guide for New Parents and Everyone Else Who Cares about Children

Kim Paleg, Ph.D.

MJF BOOKS
NEW YORK

Publisher's Note: This publication is designed to provide accurate and authoritative information in regard to the subject matter covered. It is sold with the understanding that the publisher is not engaged in rendering psychological, financial, legal, or other professional services. If expert assistance or counseling is needed, the services of a competent professional should be sought.

Published by MJF Books
Fine Communications
Two Lincoln Square
60 West 66th Street
New York, NY 10023

The Ten Things Every Parent Needs to Know
ISBN 1-56731-395-7
Copyright © 1997 by Kim Paleg

Text Design by Tracy Marie Powell

This edition published by arrangement with New Harbinger Publications, Inc.
Manufactured in the United States of America on acid-free paper
MJF Books and the MJF colophon are trademarks of Fine Creative Media, Inc.

10   9   8   7   6   5   4   3   2   1

Contents

Introduction

There's nothing more exciting than bringing a new life into the world. And the joys of being a parent keep multiplying: the first smile, the first giggle, the first time your child says Mama or Dada and means *you,* the first time your child throws his or her arms around your neck and says I love you.

This book offers a unique orientation to parenting. It supports the belief that parenting can and should be both fun and rewarding. It succinctly describes the ten general concepts essential for creating healthy relationships between parents and children. And it demonstrates how, once these concepts and their related skills are mastered, they can be applied in any situation that arises, throughout childhood and adolescence, and even into adulthood. These ten concepts are all you need to know to successfully handle the challenges of parenting while reaping the rewards.

Parenting books abound in libraries and bookstores, giving advice on everything from feeding options for newborns to dating rules for teenagers. Most of these books are filled with masses of information, strategies, and guidelines—with the implication that unless you absorb it all, you'll be unable to cope with the tasks of parenting. This book is different, and easier. Once you master the ten concepts described here (*just ten!*), you can apply them to any situation, even crises.

The concepts explored in this book include nurturing, reinforcing good behaviors, listening, expressing yourself, problem solving, choosing a coping strategy, and dealing with anger. Each chapter fully describes one of the concepts and offers examples—to ensure understanding—while accompanying exercises enable mastery of skills.

Note: The examples in the book portray a variety of parent-child situations. For purposes of simplicity, in each situation one parent is shown handling the problem alone. Although you may have an actively involved, supportive parenting partner, it's easier to conceptualize yourself handling the situation with your child.

This book, combined with your own commitment and practice, will enable you to experience all the joys and delights of parenthood along with its many challenges. If you're reading this book to improve already established relationships with your child, conscientious application of these concepts and skills should lead to noticeable improvements within a few weeks. If you are about to or have recently become a parent, this book will give you the information you need to get your relationship with your newborn off to the best possible start.

How to Nurture Your Child

According to the dictionary, *nurturing* means to provide support, encouragement, and nourishment through the stages of early development. For plants, this means daily watering, making sure there's plenty of sunlight, clearing away any weeds, and fertilizing when necessary. For children, physical nurturing includes providing food, drink, and warm clothes. It means keeping them clean and safe from danger. And it means ensuring that they get adequate sleep and plenty of cuddling.

Most parents are able to provide adequately for their children's physical needs. Emotional nurturing is equally important, and may sometimes be overlooked. Nurturing children emotionally means giving them positive attention and understanding. It means accepting and respecting who they are as individuals, and it means soothing their pain and fostering their self-esteem. Providing these essential ingredients allows children to grow into responsible, mature adults with an accurate sense of their worth and value as human beings.

The nurturing that you will learn about in this chapter is emotional nurturing; the need for it continues long past childhood. Whether you're two, twenty-two, or sixty-two, a healthy dose of emotional nurturing in your daily life enables you to thrive.

It's particularly important to provide nurturing to children because they are not born with the ability to nurture themselves. Only once they have learned good nurturing skills from their parents can they use those skills to nurture themselves. In this chapter you will learn the essential elements of nurturing your child and others with whom you share close relationships.

Six components are essential to nurturing your child:

- Attention
- Mirroring
- Understanding
- Acceptance and respect
- Soothing pain
- Fostering self-esteem

Attention

From birth, children develop their ideas of who they are and what they're worth as human beings from the way they're treated by their parents or other primary parental figures. Children need to receive these adults' attention in order to feel valued, and at an early age there is no such thing as too much attention. Attention inherently expresses interest in who they are and what they think, feel, and want.

Giving attention means spending time: playing, reading, talking, going for walks, or just doing tasks or running errands together. Giving attention means noticing: what your child is doing, saying, or needing. It means really listening when your child asks you questions or talks to you (see chapter 3 for details on listening skills).

Attention can be given by just noticing in passing and commenting on what a child is doing. By attending to children in this way, you teach them that what they have to say and what they do matters. You teach them that they're valuable. When children don't get enough of this needed attention, they may misbehave in an attempt to gain attention. To a child, even negative attention is better than no attention.

Patience is an essential component of attention. If you're really interested in what your child has to say or is capable of doing, you have to give him or her time to say or do it. Giving your time communicates your interest and that you value your child. Impatience communicates your lack of interest and that your child lacks worth in your eyes. Giving attention sounds easy, yet many busy parents spend no more than a few minutes per day really focused on their child.

Once children have learned good nurturing skills from their parents, they can use those skills to nurture themselves.

Exercise: What Is Attention?

In working to fully understand a concept, it often helps to consider your own past experiences and extrapolate from them. The following exercise uses that format, as do others in this book.

Think back to the last time someone really gave you attention, either by truly listening to something you had to say or by paying attention while you did something that was important to you. Briefly write about what was happening, who gave you the attention, what that person said or did (facial expression, gestures, tone of voice), and how you felt about yourself as a result.

What was happening? _____

_____

_____

Who gave the attention? _____

_____

_____

What did he or she actually do or say? _____

_____

_____

How did you feel about yourself? _____

_____

_____

Mirroring

Children have a tremendous need to be shown by their parents that they are wonderful and a pleasure to be around. This demonstration of delight in the child's existence is called *mirroring*. Obviously parents can't be delighted in their child every minute, but as psychologist Michael Kahn wrote, "The child looks to the parent for the answer to 'Mirror, mirror on the wall, who's the most wonderful of them all?' and needs, a reasonable percentage of the time, for the parent/mirror to answer, 'You are, my wonderful child.'"

Parents don't necessarily need to communicate this verbally. Children can learn it through nonverbal cues, such as facial expression, gesture, and tone of voice. When a mother gazes lovingly into her six-month-old's eyes, or when they play peek-a-boo, she is communicating delight in her baby's existence. When a father sees his eighteen-month-old daughter running toward him, and instinctively crouches down with outstretched arms, picks her up, whirls her around, and covers her face with kisses, he's communicating it, too.

When parents give their children enough messages that they are truly likable, lovable, and competent, they eventually no longer need to be "the most wonderful of them all." Instead, these fortunate children begin to feel confident of themselves as valuable, worthwhile humans. And they maintain the ability to nurture themselves in this way, regardless of any contradictory messages they receive from the world around them.

Understanding

Everyone, child and adult alike, needs understanding. True understanding means more than just a "Yeah, yeah, I know" response. It means seeing children and others for who they really are. True understanding requires listening to what children say, a willingness to hear their thoughts and feelings, likes and dislikes, wants and needs, hopes and dreams, fears and fantasies. It means putting aside your own expectations and assumptions about your child—your own hopes, fears, dreams, and fantasies—and really seeing your child as he or she is.

Judgment is not a part of understanding. Instead of saying "You're good" or "You're bad," you just say (verbally or otherwise) "You are who you are, and I see that *this* is who you are." Understanding means trying to get inside someone else's world in order to appreciate how it feels to be that person.

Exercise: · What Is Understanding?

Think back to the last conversation you had with someone— child or adult—in which you really tried to understand the person. In the spaces below, write down what you learned.

What did you learn about what the person thinks and feels? _____

_____

_____

_____

What did you learn about his or her likes and dislikes? _____

_____

_____

_____

What did you learn about his or her wants and needs? _____

_____

_____

_____

What did you learn about his or her hopes and dreams? _____

_____

_____

_____

What did you learn about his or her fears and fantasies? _____

_____

_____

_____

What questions might you ask that person that would give you more understanding of who they are?

1. _____

2. _____

3. _____

4. _____

5. _____

Acceptance and Respect

Mothers often state that each of their children was different from day one—and they're right. No two children are exactly alike, and the differences between them often show very early in life. Just as children are born with different genes for hair, eye, and skin color, they are also born with different temperaments.

Temperament refers to the built-in "wiring" that each child is given at (or probably before) birth—the way he or she tends to respond to or cope with life experiences. These patterns of responses tend not to change much over time. They influence how a child responds to others—and is therefore treated by others (including parents)—and how he or she performs in different arenas.

Child and family psychiatrist Stanley Turecki and writer Leslie Tonner describe nine different characteristics that determine temperament:

* Activity level—Is the child quiet and inactive, restless and very active, or somewhere in between?

* Quality of mood—Is the child essentially cheerful and optimistic, serious, or negative?

* Withdrawal—Does the child enjoy new experiences, or does he or she react instead with fear?

* Regularity—Is the child regular and predictable in his or her habits, or erratic and unpredictable?

★ Adaptability—Does the child accommodate changes easily, or does he or she have difficulty adapting?

★ Sensory threshold—Does the child tend to remain fairly calm in noisy, busy environments, or does he or she easily become overstimulated?

★ Intensity of reaction—Does the child typically react mildly to either negative or positive events, or does he or she tend instead to be loud and forceful?

Temperament is as genetically determined as physical characteristics are.

★ Distractibility—Is the child able to concentrate on a single task or subject for a long time, or is he or she easily bored, tending to daydream instead of staying focused?

★ Persistence—Does the child recover easily from setbacks or frustrations, or does his or her unhappiness persist?

Each of these characteristics represents a range. Children whose traits fall at one end of the continuum are considered "easy" children. Those whose traits fall at the other extreme are considered "difficult" children. It's important to remember that these "difficult" children *are not trying to be difficult.* They simply have a unique combination of temperamental traits that makes them inherently tougher to handle.

Each child has each of these nine traits in different proportions. That combination of traits is what makes up a child's overall temperament. Temperament is as genetically determined as physical characteristics are.

Exercise: Rating Your Temperament

Using yourself as a model, circle the number below each trait that best and most consistently describes your temperament.

1 = Easy   7 = Difficult

Activity Level

1	2	3	4	5	6	7
inactive						very active

Quality of Mood

1	2	3	4	5	6	7
cheerful						negative

Withdrawal

1	2	3	4	5	6	7
adventurous						fearful

Regularity

1	2	3	4	5	6	7
regular in habit						unpredictable

Adaptability

1	2	3	4	5	6	7
adapts easily						difficulty with transitions

Sensory Threshold

1	2	3	4	5	6	7
placid						easily overstimulated

Intensity of Reaction

1	2	3	4	5	6	7
quiet						loud

Distractibility

1	2	3	4	5	6	7
long attention span						easily distracted

Persistence

1	2	3	4	5	6	7
recovers easily						persistent in unhappiness

Of course, traits that make for an easy child aren't necessarily useful for adults, and vice versa. A quiet, placid (easy) baby can lack the persistence and drive to succeed as an adult. Nevertheless, temperament is unlikely to change much over time. You can struggle with dissatisfaction, or you can accept your traits as part of what makes you unique.

Likewise, you might wish your partner were more active and less intense, but if those are consistent traits then he or she is probably not going to change. As a parent, you might hope that your baby will be happy and mellow instead of serious and a little fussy, but if that's her temperament, well, that's who she is.

What is important in a parent-child relationship is that you can accept your child for who he or she is and respect those particular characteristics that make him or her special. Even more important is that you *communicate* that acceptance and respect to the child. Acceptance means having expectations of your child that are realistic—that fit his or her capabilities. For example, if your child is shy and quiet, it's unrealistic to expect him or her to thrive in big, noisy groups. If your child has difficulty with transitions, it's important to give lots of notice before making big changes in his or her activities or schedule.

Soothing Pain

One of the hardest things to bear is watching someone you love be in pain—whether it is your child, parent, lover, or friend. You'd probably do almost anything to prevent it. Unfortunately, pain is a part of life and everyone experiences it from time to time, even children.

Parents want to protect their children from unnecessary pain, but some pain—both physical and emotional—is inevitable. Children are going to fall down while playing. They're going to bump their heads and knees and elbows. They're going to run into bullies who pick on them for no reason. They're going to be rejected by the very child they most want for a friend. And you're not going to be able to protect them from the resulting painful feelings.

It's often easier to help children deal with physical pain than emotional pain. Physical wounds are visible and can therefore be addressed in a straight-forward way: ice packs, bandages, soothing potions, and kisses can work wonders on bumps, scrapes, and cuts. Invisible emotional wounds are more difficult to deal with and often tend to be overlooked. This is the pain that is most important, therefore, to acknowledge and soothe.

Fortunately, since life inevitably consists of struggles, it's not totally detrimental for children to experience these painful emotions. In fact, learning how to cope with the inevitable painful feelings and experiences of childhood can help your child develop the skills necessary for coping with later hardships. *Coping* means learning how to soothe the painful feelings that result from an emotional injury. You need to observe two important rules of thumb in soothing your child's pain:

★ Don't pretend your child is not in pain.

★ Don't try to solve your child's problems.

Don't pretend your child is not in pain. It is important for children to experience their feelings and to know that their feelings—whatever they may be—are OK. So it's important to acknowledge to your child that the experience hurts. "That must have hurt your feelings," "I'll bet that experience really hurt," or simply "Ouch!" are all ways of acknowledging your child's emotional pain. Just being acknowledged is soothing, and it also helps the child learn how to acknowledge his or her own feelings later on.

Don't try to solve your child's problems. Your experience probably at times enables you to see what would be helpful for your child. Nonetheless, it's important that your child be given the opportunity to learn how to solve his or her own problems. "What do you think you might do?" "How do you think you might solve this?" and "Let's think about some possible solutions" are all ways of encouraging your child to develop problem-solving skills. Not solving your child's problems doesn't mean you can't or shouldn't offer *suggestions* in the course of talking about alternatives—sometimes your child simply doesn't know all the possibilities. But solving a child's problem for him

Learning how to cope with pain can help your child develop the skills necessary for coping with later hardships.

or her communicates that he or she is incompetent or incapable of coming up with a good solution.

Fostering Self-Esteem

Most parents love their children, yet many children don't *feel* loved or worthwhile. Self-esteem is about feeling lovable and worthwhile.

People's capacity for happiness is directly related to their level of self-esteem. Self-esteem is not conceit, it's more like self-respect. It's about being calmly certain of one's worth as a person. Good self-esteem is the armor that protects against the traps of growing up: abusive relationships, sexual promiscuity, drug and alcohol abuse. It gives a person the reason and strength to resist peer pressure.

Self-image—good or bad—isn't established overnight or as the result of a single incident. It's the accumulated result of many, many interactions and incidents over many years. Even as adults, self-image is open to enhancement by positive interactions and is vulnerable to the ravages of negative interactions.

Parents need to do several things on an ongoing basis to foster self-esteem in their children:

* Help the child feel lovable and worthwhile by mirroring, cherishing his or her uniqueness, and providing unconditional love. This doesn't mean liking or accepting all your child's behavior. It means separating the person from the behavior (see chapter 6).

* Provide focused attention (see above).

* Listen to and accept the child's full range of feelings, including the painful and angry ones (see chapter 3).

⭐ Express your own feelings honestly and appropriately (see chapter 4).

⭐ Understand, accept, and respect who the child really is (see above).

⭐ Give the child the freedom to grow and develop at his or her own pace by keeping your expectations in line with the child's current capabilities.

⭐ Discipline respectfully, by providing clear, understandable, and consistent rules. This means reinforcing (praising) the child's positive behavior, the absence of negative behavior, and any efforts made toward a goal—not just achievements (see chapter 2). Disciplining also involves giving the child choices, consistent and appropriate consequences without anger, and problem-solving opportunities (see chapters 6 and 7).

In every interaction you have with your child lies an underlying message about your child's lovableness and worth as a person. Over time, these messages influence how your child views him- or herself, his or her self-esteem. This chapter and the rest of the book address the skills that will allow you to foster more healthy relationships. By learning and practicing these skills, you will be able to ensure your child's best possible self-image.

Many components make up the nurturing your child needs. Giving attention provides the message that the child is important, and that what he or she says and does matters. Mirroring teaches your child that he or she is lovable, likable, and a delight to be around. Understanding allows the child to experience really being seen. And accepting and respecting the child's unique characteristics gives the message that what is seen is OK. Helping the child soothe his or her pain communicates that he or she is a competent person.

A child who is given these and the essential ingredients of self-esteem will thrive as surely as a plant that is regularly exposed to the sun, watered, fertilized, and cleared of weeds.

Keys to Nurturing Your Child

- ★ Give your child positive attention.
- ★ Mirror your delight in his or her existence.
- ★ Show understanding, acceptance, and respect for who he or she is.
- ★ Help your child learn to soothe his or her pain.
- ★ Foster his or her self-esteem.

2

How to Find and Reinforce the Good

A belief that is fairly prevalent in America holds that criticizing someone enough will cause them to work at improving themselves. This chapter will discuss the problems with this assumption and describe more effective ways of encouraging desired behavior in children. The central concept here is that of positive reinforcement.

Before looking at how reinforcement works between parents and children, let's look at the concept of reinforcement generally. Take a minute to do a quick exercise on how reinforcement affects you in your work life.

Exercise: Understanding Reinforcement

Think about your last week of work, including work around the house. List the tasks you remember doing really well, that you felt satisfied with.

_____

_____

_____

Now list the tasks with which you remember feeling dissatisfied.

_____

_____

_____

Which tasks were easier to remember? Those you were satisfied or unsatisfied with? _____

_____

If you're like most people, you remembered the tasks that you were dissatisfied with more easily than those with which you were satisfied.

Now think about your other experiences on the job and at home.

Do you receive more recognition when you do something well or when you make a mistake? _____ _____

Is more attention paid to you when you're doing your job quietly, not questioning the status quo, or when you protest or criticize? _____ _____

Is it true that "the squeaky wheel gets the grease"? _____

Next write a brief description of a recent incident in which you felt proud of yourself. _____

_____

_____

Now write a brief description of a time when you felt bad about yourself (ashamed, discouraged, embarrassed, guilty, or humiliated).

_____

_____

_____

Which incident was easiest to remember and describe? Positive or negative?

_____

Which felt more significant? Positive or negative? _____

Does the positive incident or the negative incident seem most representative of how you see yourself? _____

Again, if you're like many people, the negative incident was easier to remember. And of the two, the negative incident probably took more of your attention and felt more significant and personally meaningful.

Before leaving these last two incidents, close your eyes and try to remember how you felt in each of the situations. When you were right in the middle of feeling proud of yourself, did it seem harder or easier to imagine doing even better in the future? Take your time to really feel it. Harder or easier? _____

When you were feeling bad about yourself, did it seem harder or easier to imagine doing even better in the future? Take your time to really feel it. Harder or easier? _____

Positive Reinforcement

The myth mentioned at the beginning of the chapter states that if you want someone to do better, you just have to focus on all the ways that the person isn't doing well enough. Although this approach occasionally yields some short-term improvement, the long-term result is more often a decrease in that person's self-esteem and a corresponding decrease in his or her motivation for doing better. How does this apply to parent-child relationships? Specifically, how do you encourage your children to behave better if the standard approach of focusing on their misbehavior doesn't work and isn't appropriate?

To answer this question, you first need to understand the concept of reinforcement. When someone is rewarded for behaving in a particular way, they're more likely to behave that way again. If you were given ten dollars every time you did a load of laundry, you'd probably do the laundry more frequently. When a three-year-old is given a sticker every time she brushes her teeth, she's likely to brush her teeth more consistently. That reward is called a *reinforcer,* and the process of giving the reinforcer is called *reinforcement.*

A reinforcer is anything that increases the chances that a behavior will be repeated. Reinforcers don't need to be, and often are not, material objects. They can be anything, and what works for one person won't necessarily work for another. Stickers might work for most three-year-olds, but they're unlikely to work for a ten-year-old. One reinforcer that works consistently for children of all ages is *attention*: Behavior that is noticed is more likely to be repeated than behavior that is ignored.

Positive attention consists of many things, including a smile, a wink, a hug, a caress, and a few appreciative or encouraging words. However, even negative attention—a slap, an angry reprimand—can be reinforcing to a child, particularly when positive attention is in short supply. *Any* attention can feel better than none simply because it affirms the child's existence. This is another crucial reason why focusing only on your child's misbehavior is not an effective way to improve his or her behavior. Attention—even if it's painful—can act as reinforcement, with the result that the misbehavior will be repeated.

So the key to encouraging your child to behave better is to find (recognize) and reinforce his or her good behavior. There are four steps to this:

1. Ignore the misbehavior (unless it presents a danger to your child or someone else).

2. Find behaviors you feel OK about.

3. Reinforce those behaviors with positive attention.

4. Gradually start reinforcing only those behaviors you want repeated.

Step 1: Ignore the Misbehavior

Focusing primarily on how your child is misbehaving will negatively affect his or her self-esteem and, consequently, lower his or her motivation for change. Furthermore, because yelling, scolding, and slapping constitute attention—albeit negative attention—they can reinforce misbehavior. Even when your intention is to stop a particular behavior, you could be inadvertently reinforcing it. This is one of the major difficulties with punishment (as will be discussed in chapter 7 on choices and consequences): Punishment can actually be experienced as a reinforcement. To lower the frequency of negative behavior, it must not be reinforced. It must be *ignored.*

Positive attention includes a smile, a wink, a hug, a caress, and a few encouraging words.

Unfortunately, ignoring misbehavior is often more easily said than done. When someone misbehaves only occasionally, it's possible to occasionally ignore the behavior. But when someone seems to misbehave constantly, it's much more difficult.

Note that when you first start ignoring a misbehavior, you may see a temporary increase, rather than a decrease, in the frequency of the misbehavior. Everyone likes familiarity, especially children, and although the old pattern that focused on the misbehavior may not have felt good to your child, it was familiar and predictable. When you stop behaving so predictably, your child may attempt to elicit the familiar response by increasing the misbehavior. Try to remember that the increase is normal, and stick to your decision to ignore it. Consistency is crucial when you're learning new skills.

Caution: Ignoring the misbehavior doesn't mean looking away when your two-year-old sticks a fork into the electrical outlet or your five-year-old plays on top of a retaining wall with a twenty-foot drop onto concrete. Nor does it mean not noticing when your thirteen-year-old finds your handgun or your prescription pills. Clearly, when the behavior is dangerous, you have to take action to stop it, and the action has to be immediate.

✳ *Juanita and Marco's Story* ✳

Four-year-old Marco seemed to stop whining only when he slept. It drove his mother, Juanita, crazy, but she realized that every time she answered his whining she was giving it attention. So she decided to try to ignore it. She told Marco that she'd only answer him when he spoke to her in a nice voice and would ignore him otherwise. It took many days of consistency—and some occasional reminders ("I can't hear you when you talk to me in that tone of voice.")—but eventually Marco began whining less often.

✳ *Scott and Cameron's Story* ✳

Scott's two-year-old son, Cameron, was always into things he shouldn't be. Although he found it impossible to ignore Cameron's misbehavior altogether, Scott developed a modified strategy of distracting and redirecting. Every time Cameron would pick up a pen and head toward the wall, Scott would intercept him. While carrying Cameron to his drawing table, Scott would say firmly, "Pens are for drawing on paper only." He didn't focus on the misbehavior. He just clearly stated the boundary and then redirected him. When Cameron would start tearing the pages of the book he was looking at, Scott would gently remove the book while saying, "Books are for reading, not for tearing." Then he would give Cameron some newspaper to tear up.

At bedtime, Cameron found a million things that he just "had" to do before putting on his pajamas or brushing his teeth. Scott was usually exhausted by the time he'd redirected Cameron to the task at hand so many times. Rarely did Cameron go to bed without a tantrum. Although Scott was not able to actually ignore the misbehavior, he did avoid focusing on it. And over time he began seeing changes that reinforced his own ability to persevere.

Chapter 4, on expressing yourself, and chapter 7, on choices and consequences, describe in more detail the skills necessary for managing misbehaviors with a minimum of attention.

Anne and Raelene's Story

Twelve-year-old Raelene was a preteen "teenager." She barely spoke to her mother, Anne, responding mostly with grunts and occasional monosyllables—or not responding at all. She spent much of her time at home alone in her room and projected an air of detachment and mild contempt for the family.

It infuriated Anne that Raelene didn't answer her courteously or help out more around the house. The anger and frustration she felt translated into sarcastic comments to Raelene as well as constant requests for help. If anything, these responses seemed to provoke further detachment and contempt. Recognizing this, Anne decided to try to ignore Raelene's provocative behavior and not respond with her usual anger and frustration.

Step 2: Find Behaviors You Feel OK About

To reinforce the behaviors that you want, you have to first recognize those behaviors. Initially it may seem impossible to notice anything other than the behaviors you don't like, but it's important to make an effort to find any and all behaviors that you feel OK—or even neutral—about. Even a neutral behavior is more desirable than a negative behavior. Don't look for perfection, just for what's OK. In particular, look for small behaviors rather than big, obvious behaviors.

Juanita and Marco

Juanita hated Marco's whining, but when she really tried hard, she was able to see that he did have his occasional quieter moments. He was quieter when he ate, when he listened to her read to him, and sometimes, though not often, when he drew with his favorite marking pens. She would have liked more of that quiet time, but what she found was good enough to start with.

Scott and Cameron

Scott wanted Cameron to stop having so many temper tantrums throughout the day—especially at bedtime. So on the rare occasions when Cameron brushed his teeth, got into his pajamas, or went to bed with only a small fuss rather than his usual tantrum, it was worth noticing—even when he'd had three tantrums earlier in the day.

✴ *Anne and Raelene* ✴

Anne worked hard to find behaviors that she liked in Raelene's repertoire. She definitely preferred it when Raelene answered a question—even if with only a grunt or monosyllable—than when she didn't bother answering at all. And Anne noticed that Raelene did sometimes take her dinner plate to the sink before heading back upstairs to her room.

Step 3: Reinforce Those Behaviors with Positive Attention

Behavior that is reinforced is more likely to be repeated than behavior that is ignored. Reinforcement, by definition, is anything that makes a behavior more likely to be repeated. With both children and adults, attention—either positive (a warm smile, a hug, a wink, a caress, an appreciative comment) or negative (a critical comment, a scolding)—is the most reliable reinforcement.

✴ *Juanita and Marco* ✴

Marco whined so much that initially his mother simply reinforced him every time he was silent. When he had his mouth full of food, Juanita would give him a quick hug. When he spent two minutes engrossed in drawing, she said, "I love to see you enjoying yourself drawing." When he listened quietly to a book being read to him, she said, "I enjoy reading to you when you listen so well." Marco began to spend more quiet time in activities, although when he spoke it was sometimes still in a whiny voice.

★   *Scott and Cameron*   ★

Whenever Scott noticed Cameron doing *anything* other than misbehaving—including running around the house making engine noises, pretending to be an airplane—he tried also to reinforce the behavior. When Cameron took out his blocks, before he had a chance to start throwing them around, his father made a point of saying "It looks like you're going to have fun building today." When Cameron started looking at his books, before he had the opportunity to tear any of the pages, Scott made an effort to reinforce the behavior with a positive comment.

★   *Anne and Raelene*   ★

Anne decided to focus on reinforcing the two behaviors she had identified as acceptable. Every time Raelene responded to her mother, even with a grunt, Anne said simply, "Thanks." When Raelene took her plate to the kitchen, Anne said, "Thanks, sweetie," as Raelene headed upstairs. After a while Raelene began responding more frequently, and occasionally even answering more or less politely.

She began more frequently to take her plate to the kitchen, though she still rarely took anything in addition to her plate.

Step 4: Gradually Start Reinforcing Only Those Behaviors You Want Repeated

Anything other than the negative behaviors is worth noticing—and reinforcing—at first. When the frequency of neutral and positive behaviors increases, you can begin choosing which specific behaviors you want to continue reinforcing.

✶ *Juanita and Marco* ✶

Juanita decided to focus on reinforcing Marco only when he spoke to her in a nice tone of voice, rather than to continue reinforcing every behavior other than whining, including his silent periods. She still occasionally gave attention to those quiet times, but primarily she waited until he spoke to her nicely. Then she would answer him and add "and I really appreciate your tone of voice."

✶ *Scott and Cameron* ✶

Scott decided to start reinforcing Cameron only when he played for more than a minute without throwing, breaking, or tearing whatever he was playing with. He decided to start with one minute, and then gradually to increase the time he waited before giving a reinforcement. At those times, Scott told Cameron, "I really like how you're playing with those blocks," or crayons, books, cars, etc. When Cameron went to bed without his usual tantrum, his father said, "I really enjoyed being with you tonight," and gave him an extra goodnight squeeze.

⭐ *Anne and Raelene* ⭐

Eventually Anne decided to stop reinforcing Raelene's every response and to reinforce only the polite ones. Similarly, she began to thank Raelene only when she took something to the sink in addition to her plate—her glass, her silverware. Eventually, Anne became even more selective and reinforced Raelene only when she took some dishes in addition to the ones she herself had used.

Exercise: Developing Your Plan

1. Ignore the misbehavior. In the space provided below, describe a misbehavior that you would like to decrease or eliminate from your child's behavioral repertoire. Pick a fairly frequent behavior that is consistently annoying to you. (Remember, this approach does not apply to behaviors that are potentially dangerous. Those behaviors must be handled immediately, not gradually.)

_____

_____

_____

Now describe how you usually respond to this misbehavior.

_____

_____

_____

Describe how you plan to ignore—or avoid focusing on—the misbehavior.

_____

_____

_____

Note: Remember that when you start ignoring the misbehavior it might temporarily increase in frequency. This is perfectly normal, though frustrating. Just stick with your plan.

2. Find behaviors that you feel OK about. This is the hardest step: finding behaviors that don't irritate or annoy you or that you even feel good about. Look for small behaviors rather than big, obvious behaviors. Look for exceptions to your child's usual misbehavior: When he's sleepy does he race around less? When she's refreshed does she talk in a less whiny voice? Look at what occurs just before the misbehavior. Is the first step of the chain of behaviors in fact OK? For instance, tearing pages out of books isn't OK, but what about picking up a book to look at? Don't look for perfection, just for what's OK.

In the space below, write down some of your child's behaviors that you feel OK about.

_____

_____

_____

3. Reinforce those behaviors with positive attention. In the space provided, write how you will reinforce the behaviors listed above. Remember that positive attention can include both verbal statements, such as "I really like how you are [state the OK behavior]," as well as nonverbal gestures, such as a smile, a hug, a kiss, or a caress.

_____

_____

_____

4. Gradually start reinforcing only those behaviors you want repeated. Some of the behaviors you listed as feeling neutral or OK are probably just tolerable, whereas you'd actually like some of the others to occur more frequently. In the space below, write down the behaviors that you will eventually focus on reinforcing

_____

_____

_____

Be aware that this may require a series of steps toward your ultimate goal. For example, if you're trying to encourage your child to clean up his or her toys, you might initially reinforce anything getting put anywhere near its correct place. Then you might only reinforce anything actually getting put in its correct place. Next you might only reinforce two or three things getting put in their correct places, and so forth.

Remember that change takes time and nothing will happen overnight. You may need to experiment with reinforcements to find those that work most effectively with your particular child—one child will like to have her hair tousled affectionately, while another will hate it.

What is perhaps most important is that you see reinforcement as a tool for improving your relationship with your child rather than as a way of manipulating your child's behavior. Reinforcement is a way to let your child know that you like something he or she is doing and that you'd like to see it more frequently.

It's also extremely important to recognize that every child has some behaviors that are worth reinforcing and to begin with finding and reinforcing them. Reinforcement makes children feel good and increases their desire to please you. It's a lot more effective than criticism, and it's a lot healthier for their self-image.

Once you establish the pattern of using reinforcements that work, you can then gradually encourage the particular behaviors that you want increased. When you combine these skills with those of giving choices and setting consequences (see chapter 7), you'll have the start of an effective toolkit for engaging cooperation and positive behavior.

Keys to Finding and Reinforcing the Good

★ Ignore the misbehavior (unless it presents a danger to your child or someone else).

★ Find behaviors you feel OK about.

★ Reinforce those behaviors using positive attention.

★ Gradually start reinforcing only those behaviors you want repeated.

3

How to Listen to Your Child

Everyone assumes that they listen—and of course everyone does listen, to some extent. You hear your partner say he or she is going to bed. You hear your friend tell you the time of her dinner party on Saturday night. Most people even think of themselves as good listeners. However real listening is much more difficult—and more rare—than many people realize. In this chapter you will learn to appreciate the importance of listening as a fundamental building block in your relationship with your child. You will learn the ten roadblocks to good listening and the three steps that ensure good listening.

✳ *Devon's Story* ✳

Ten-year-old Devon and her father were eating dinner.
Devon had been unusually quiet. "What's up, sweetie?" her father
asked. Devon shook her head but remained silent. Devon's father
persisted, "It must be something, you look like misery personified."
"Terry and I had a fight," Devon responded quietly. Her father
snorted, "Is that all? I thought it must be something serious. You and
Terry fight so much it's hard to believe you're still friends. Why do
you bother with her?" Softly Devon said, "It's OK. It's nothing. Excuse
me, I have to go finish my homework."

✳ *Kelly's Story* ✳

Seven-year-old Kelly's aunt Sarah was picking Kelly up
from her after-school program. As she opened the car door, Sarah
asked, "How was school?" "Awful," Kelly responded, "I couldn't find
some homework and my teacher yelled at me in front of the whole
class. I was so embarrassed . . ." Sarah cut in: "Sounds awful. You
know what I'd do? I'd do the homework over again tonight and then
first thing tomorrow morning I'd go give it to her and apologize. I
might even tell her how awful it was being yelled at. Or if you like, I
could go and talk to her for you." "I don't want . . ." Kelly began, but
her aunt interrupted again. "Well, don't you worry, honey, we'll take
care of it."

Blocks to Listening

Unfortunately, you've probably had experiences similar to those of Devon and Kelly, where no real listening occurred. Yet listening is one of the most important elements in any good relationship, whether it's between a child and parent, lovers, friends, colleagues, or employer and employee. Real listening is more than just being quiet while the other person talks. Real listening implies that you want to understand what the other person is saying—and therefore what that person thinks, feels, and needs. It means putting aside your own ideas and judgments long enough to really hear. This is difficult, and as a result, many people engage instead in "pseudo-listening" where the intention is not really to understand but to appear to be listening. Pseudo-listening can involve the use of any of the following ten blocks to listening:

- Mind reading
- Rehearsing
- Filtering
- Judging
- Daydreaming
- Advising
- Sparring
- Being right
- Derailing
- Placating

Mind reading. If you pay more attention to what you think someone "really means" (based primarily on your own feelings, assumptions, or hunches) than to what he or she is actually saying, then you are mind reading. For instance, when Sally told her dad that she was too tired to go to the ball game and preferred instead to stay home and watch a video, he "knew" that she "really meant" that she was angry at him and was punishing him.

Real listening implies that you want to understand what the other person is saying—and therefore what that person thinks, feels, and needs.

Rehearsing. Rehearsing occurs when you mentally plan your response to what someone is saying to you instead of really listening to the person. For example, when Philip was telling his mother why he wanted to go with his friends to the concert, instead of listening, she was running through all the reasons she couldn't afford the ticket.

Filtering. When you filter, you may tune out certain topics or you may hear only certain things and tune out everything else. For instance, Peggy used filtering to listen for—and react to—any possible hint of unhappiness in seven-year-old Julia's conversations, no matter what else she said. Julia, on the other hand, filtered out anything her mom said that had to do with her absent father.

Judging. You are judging if you decide ahead of time that the other person is not worth hearing (because he or she is stupid, crazy, hypocritical, immature), and that therefore you will listen only in order to confirm your opinion. For example, fifteen-year-old David thought that his dad was a loser, and listened only to the things his father said that supported that judgment.

Daydreaming. If you daydream, you pay only a fraction of your attention to the person talking—inside your thoughts are wandering in other directions. For instance, while Francie was talking about her homework, her dad drifted into fantasies of starting his own business.

Advising. Jumping in with advice when the other person has barely stopped talking (or before) is a sign that you are advising rather than listening. "Fixing things" may not even be what the other person wants. For example, when ten-year-old Peter was telling his older sister about how he felt used by his best friend, she couldn't wait until he finished talking to start giving advice: "You shouldn't let him do that to you. Just tell him to bug off. When he calls to ask you to do something for him, tell him you're too busy. Or better yet, let the machine answer the call and then don't call him back."

Sparring. If you listen only enough to find something to disagree with, then assert your position—regardless of what the other person says—you are sparring. Sparring can include sarcasm and put-downs. For instance, when Joan was explaining why she wasn't enjoying being on the swim team anymore, her father started pointing out all the flaws in her reasoning. It didn't matter what Joan said, her father had a conflicting opinion about it.

Being right. If you go to great lengths to avoid the suggestion that you're wrong—including lying, shouting, twisting the facts, changing the subject, making excuses, and accusing—then you are not listening. For example, when five-year-old Kathy said she thought it was mean of her mom not to let her watch the end of the movie, her mother responded, "That's not mean. Besides, you already watched most of it. Anyway, you're obviously cranky today so I probably shouldn't even have let you watch as much as you did."

Derailing. If you change the subject or make a joke whenever you become bored or uncomfortable with the conversation you are guilty of derailing. For instance, every time Patty began expressing her concerns to her son about his grades, he laughed it off or started talking about something else.

Placating. If you're so concerned with being nice, agreeable, or liked that you agree with everything being said without really listening, you are placating. Raoul was helping his younger brother, Thom, with a science project. Thom was so happy with the attention, he agreed with whatever Raoul suggested, whether or not it fit the project description.

Exercise: Identifying Blocks to Listening

Go back to the two stories at the beginning of the chapter and try to identify which blocks to listening were being used. Then, next to each of the names below, write the block or blocks you identified.

Devon _____

Kelly _____

In the first example, Devon's father completely *derailed* the discussion from any serious consideration of his daughter's feelings. Either he didn't want to waste time on what he considered boring and trivial or he was uncomfortable with how upset Devon appeared.

In the second story, Sarah was *advising* Kelly almost before she had finished speaking. Sarah didn't even consider whether her niece might have her own ideas about solving the problem.

When you really want someone to listen to you, being judged or derailed or getting unsolicited advice doesn't feel good, nor does it make you want to keep talking.

Exercise: What Is Listening?

Answer the following questions in the space provided.

Think about an occasion in your past when you tried unsuccessfully to tell someone (a partner, friend, parent, or colleague) something important. What was that person's response? _____

_____

_____

Did that person's response make you want to continue talking with him or her, telling more about your feelings and thoughts? Or were you frustrated, disappointed, or angry? _____

_____

_____

What blocks to listening did that person use? _____

_____

Is this a fairly consistent pattern of response from that person? _____

If so, this may be his or her style of listening.

How did this response make you feel about your relationship with that person? About yourself and the things you had to say? _____

_____

_____

_____

Is there someone in your life who really listens to what you have to say? What does that person do that makes you feel good? _____

_____

_____

_____

Exercise: Listening Practice

Consider this situation: It's 5:30 and the office is clearing out fast. You spent an extra few minutes searching for a misplaced file, and now the corridors are almost empty. As you hurry across the parking lot to your car, a casual friend catches up to walk with you. You like this person and have tried to encourage the friendship. You slow your pace and exchange small talk as you continue walking. Then the friend says, "Look, I'm in big trouble. I need to talk to you. Can you give me some time?"

You've barely nodded before your friend starts pouring out the story: "It's my son, my fifteen-year-old. I think he's using drugs or something. Last night when he came home there was something weird about his eyes. And it's not the first time I've thought that. When I asked him about it, he got really angry, started swearing at me and actually shoved me against the wall as he went past. Now I'm scared to raise it with him again. He's strong and I don't feel safe. But I'm scared to ignore it, too. I don't know what I should do."

You want to be helpful. Using the first response that comes to mind, write down what you would say to your friend. _____

_____

_____

Now think about the person you described in the preceding exercise, the one who really listens to you and makes you feel good. What would he or she say to your friend? Using that person as a guide, write down the most helpful response you can think of. _____

_____

_____

Compare the two responses. Which do you think would feel the most supportive or helpful? Was your initial, automatic response similar to the kinds of responses you have encountered in the past, either as a child or more recently? Because it's familiar, you can respond this way automatically even when you know from your own experience that it's not really helpful. Similarly, even when you know what it's like to feel really listened to, you may not know exactly how to do it for someone else.

Listening Skills

So what will enable your child to feel really heard and acknowledged? There are three major rules to observe in giving a helpful response:

- ★ Listen with your full attention—instead of half-listening.

- ★ Attend to the feelings as well as to the words.

- ★ Actively acknowledge that you've heard.

Listen with your full attention. This is probably the hardest of the three rules to accomplish, because it really means *full* attention. It means putting down the newspaper or book you're reading or the magazine you're leafing through. It means turning off the television program or the video game you're involved in. It means ignoring the urge to minimize, criticize, analyze, or solve the presented problem. It means letting go of the tendency to think ahead about what your response is going to be rather than just listening.

Part of paying attention is *showing* that you're listening. Maintaining eye contact, nodding, leaning forward slightly, smiling or frowning in sympathy with what is being said can all be important in helping your child feel heard, and conveying that he or she has your full attention. With a small child, you might need to physically get down to his or her level so that you can make eye contact.

Attend to the feelings as well as to the words. Understanding the feelings underlying the message may take some practice. It's important to remember that listening to and acknowledging your child's feelings doesn't mean that you have to agree with those feelings. Nor do you have to share them. You do, however, need to be aware of them, and that takes empathy—the ability to put yourself in the other person's shoes and imagine their feelings. Pay attention to the nonverbal messages: facial expression, tone of voice, body posture, and so on. Try to picture how you might feel under similar circumstances.

In the beginning, and especially with young children, you might want to simply use as your guide the four basic feeling categories: glad, mad, sad, and bad. Glad contains all the positive feelings: happy, confident, proud, cheerful, delighted. Mad includes feelings such as angry, resentful, annoyed, furious, and frustrated. Sad feelings include disappointed, gloomy, lonely, miserable, vulnerable, and despairing. Bad includes any feelings that don't fit the other categories: afraid, bored, confused, desperate, embarrassed, guilty, helpless, needy, panicky, trapped, worried, and so forth. When you can identify which of the four main categories the feelings fit into, it might help to run through a bigger list of fairly typical feelings to identify the feeling more closely. Now take a look at the list on the following page to use as a guide.

It's important to remember that listening to and acknowledging your child's feelings doesn't mean that you have to agree with those feelings.

Sometimes, no matter how hard you try, you still won't fully understand what your child is experiencing. Young children can at times be almost unintelligible when they express themselves. Older children can also get too caught up in their feelings to make total sense. You've probably experienced times yourself when you weren't as coherent as you would have liked. Sometimes you just need more information in order to understand and acknowledge what the other person is saying. The basic rule of thumb at

Feelings List

Glad	**Mad**	**Sad**	**Bad**
Amused	Angry	Defeated	Afraid
Cheerful	Annoyed	Dejected	Anxious
Confident	Enraged	Depressed	Bored
Delighted	Frustrated	Despairing	Confused
Excited	Furious	Disappointed	Desperate
Grateful	Impatient	Discouraged	Embarrassed
Happy	Irked	Gloomy	Guilty
Pleased	Irritated	Hopeless	Helpless
Proud	Livid	Lonely	Horrified
Relieved	Resentful	Miserable	Isolated
Satisfied	Violated	Pessimistic	Needy
Secure		Resigned	Overwhelmed
Thrilled		Unappreciated	Panicky
		Unfulfilled	Pressured
		Unloved	Stuck
		Vulnerable	Threatened
			Trapped
			Uneasy
			Upset
			Worried

these times is to *ask*. Ask for clarification. Ask for more information. When you understand, then you can acknowledge.

Actively acknowledge that you've heard. This is the final rule for listening. Acknowledging doesn't mean agreeing, and it doesn't preclude limiting the behavior (for example, it is OK for your child to be angry, but not for him to swear at you or to kick the walls). Acknowledging does mean letting your child know verbally that you've heard what's been said—both the content and the feeling.

It's often hard to acknowledge angry or painful feelings. The key thing to remember is that you are showing respect for those feelings—you aren't necessarily agreeing with them. Acknowledgment can range from a simple expression such as "That's too bad!" "Ouch!" or "What a nightmare!" to more complex statements that paraphrase, or restate in your own words, the content and feelings expressed by your child, for example:

"You really sound confused about which class to take."

"I can see how sad you are about Dad and I having split up."

"You sound really hopeless, as if nothing you do will resolve the problem with Becky."

"It sounds like you're really worried that if this scholarship doesn't come through you won't be able to go to college at all. You'll have to go to work."

For simple interactions, the simple responses work well. But for more important interactions, where it's important to you that your child feels really heard and acknowledged, use paraphrasing. Once you've listened to and acknowledged what your child is saying to you, it may be time for you to give *feedback*, your reaction to what he or she has said. Feedback must be immediate, honest, and supportive. *Immediate* means that you give your response as soon as possible, without delay. *Honest* means that you give your real reaction, revealing your own feelings, without fear of offending. *Supportive* means stating your honest response in ways that are tolerable to hear rather than deliberately hurtful or brutal. "I'm disappointed that you didn't check with me first" is more supportive than "That was damn stupid and irresponsible of you!" (Chapter 4, "How to Express Yourself," goes into more detail about this.)

Let's go back to the two stories at the beginning of the chapter and look at how each situation might have evolved if the three rules of listening had been observed.

✦   *Devon*   ✦

Devon and her father were eating dinner together. Devon was clearly unhappy—her father had correctly heard that feeling. However, her father was either bored with hearing about the frequent fights between Devon and her friend or uncomfortable with the depth of Devon's feelings. Thus he trivialized those feelings—and, in fact, the entire relationship between Devon and her friend Terry. If Devon's father had been willing or able to fully listen to and acknowledge Devon, the interaction might have gone more like this:

Father: What's up, sweetie?

Devon shakes her head but remains silent.

Father (persisting): It must be something, you look like misery personified.

Devon (quietly): Terry and I had a fight.

Father: You seem pretty torn up about this one.

Devon: Yeah. We've had fights before, but we could still be friends. This one feels different—more serious. I mean, we said some awful things to each other. I don't get it. I'm scared about what it means.

Father: It's scary to suddenly think of losing your best friend.

Devon: Yeah. I can't imagine it—and I don't understand it. *(Long pause)* I guess I'll have to wait and see how things go. Maybe we need some time to cool off. Anyway, I need to go do my homework. Catch you later.

The experience of being heard and acknowledged was tremendously beneficial to both Devon and the relationship between her and her father. Even though Devon's father thought that the two friends fought entirely too much, he didn't let that get in the way of listening to Devon. And although he guessed that this too would blow over for them, he was willing to acknowledge Devon's pain and fear.

Kelly

As you will recall, the second situation involved Kelly and her aunt Sarah after a bad day at school. Sarah could barely wait for the words to leave Kelly's mouth before she started bombarding her with unasked-for advice and solving her problems. Sarah was so caught up in thinking about what *she* would do that there was no way she could pay full attention to what Kelly was saying. Had she done so, the conversation would have been very different.

Sarah: How was school?

Kelly: Awful. I couldn't find some homework and my teacher yelled at me in front of the whole class. I was so embarrassed.

Sarah (sympathetically): Sounds awful.

Kelly: It was. But then I found it—in the wrong folder—so I didn't have to stay late. But she didn't even apologize for yelling at me. I hate her!

Sarah: You've had a hard time with her, haven't you?

Kelly: Yeah. It's funny though—she's actually nicer to me than to a lot of the others. No one likes her. It's good the year is almost over. I can't wait to get out of her class.

Again, the situation ends completely differently when Kelly's aunt curbs her tendency to give advice and solve others' problems, and simply listens and acknowledges. Sarah discovered that Kelly didn't really need her advice after all. Kelly had already taken care of the immediate problem and was looking forward to the more permanent solution of a new year and new teacher.

Exercise: Applying the Three Rules of Listening

Look back to the two responses you wrote in the previous exercise to the hypothetical friend who was having trouble with his or her son. Determine which, if any, of the three rules of listening were followed in each of the responses. If there was listening with full attention, write *Attention* next to the response. If the feelings were attended to, write *Feelings* next to the response. If there was active acknowledgment, write *Acknowledgment* next to the response.

Now develop a response that includes all three rules of listening.

_____

_____

_____

Your response might look something like one of these:

> "Gosh, that does sound scary. Especially if you think your son might get violent again. How can I help?"

> "What a nightmare! No wonder you're scared to raise the subject again—or to ignore it. Maybe we could go somewhere and explore the different options."

> "The idea of your son using drugs is really frightening. If you don't know what to do, I wonder whether it would help to talk with the Employee Assistance Program counselor in the office? I'd be happy to go with you if you'd like."

Each of these three example responses involves giving full attention to your friend's scared feelings as well as to the request for help, and then acknowledging that you have heard with a statement of support and an offer of assistance.

As you may have gathered, the actual words you use in listening and acknowledging are not the most important factor. What is crucial is to let your child know that you think what he or she is saying is important enough to demand your full attention—not only to the words but also to the feelings. By acknowledging what is said, you let your child know that you really do want to understand. This not only bolsters self-esteem, but it makes it easier for your child to trust you and therefore to risk talking with you again.

Keys to Listening to Your Child

★ Listen with your full attention.

★ Attend to the feelings as well as to the words.

★ Actively acknowledge that you've heard.

4

How to Express Yourself

Everyone expresses themselves all the time. It's impossible not to express yourself. On a fundamental level, everything you say, every action you take, is driven by your needs—those things essential to your physical or emotional survival. Physical sensations—hunger, thirst, fatigue—drive certain decisions. Emotional needs—for affection, to feel in control, to have a sense of belonging—drive others. On a more obvious level, everything you say and do directly or indirectly expresses something about who you are in terms of your likes, dislikes, thoughts, feelings, and wants. Each time you make a choice, each time you state an opinion, each time you react to something, you express some part of yourself.

It's probably clear by now that when your child is upset the best thing you can do is listen. But what about when you're upset? What can you do when you don't like your child's behavior? How can you deal with your own painful or angry feelings? What about your needs? In this chapter you will learn the three major rules for expressing yourself in the most useful (healthy) way, as well as the various dos and don'ts.

✳ *Carey and Sean's Story* ✳

Carey hated it when her six-year-old son, Sean, left his jacket and shoes laying on the kitchen floor after school. If she put them away for him, she felt exploited and resentful. On the other hand, if she left them there, she had to step over them several times in preparing dinner. Although she'd yelled at Sean many times to put them away himself, and threatened dire consequences if he didn't, nothing changed.

✳ *Maddy and Erin's Story* ✳

Maddy was always exhausted by the time she got home. Three days a week she worked long hours as an oncology nurse and then picked up her nine-year-old, Jamie, from after-school care before returning home. On those days, Maddy's fifteen-year-old daughter, Erin, was supposed to have dinner ready by the time they arrived. Recently, Erin had started hanging out after school at a local bookstore where a boy she liked worked. Dinner was rarely prepared on time, and its quality was less than predictable. The situation was becoming intolerable to Maddy.

Engaging Cooperation

The best way to get your child's cooperation in making changes is to express how you feel about the offending behavior and what you want done about it. Children don't usually want their parents to be unhappy. They may be unaware of the impact of their behavior on you, or the pursuit of their own needs may simply take precedence over their consideration of your feelings. When you express what you feel and what you want and need, you give your child essential information. With that information, your child can decide whether to keep doing the behavior in question or whether to make other choices.

Sometimes just describing the situation is enough to solve the problem.

Three steps are essential in expressing yourself:

1. Describe the situation.

2. Use an *I* statement to describe your feelings.

3. Describe what you want or need in the situation.

Describe the situation. The first step in expressing yourself is to describe the situation, giving the information necessary to explain why it's a problem for you: "Peter, the dog's dish is empty and he hasn't been fed all day." "The peanut butter and jelly jars are on the counter, Carol, with the lids off, and the ants are starting to gather." "Rory, it's almost noon and we're due at the rehearsal at 12:15." Notice that all these descriptions begin with a statement of the situation, followed by an explanation of why the situation is potentially a problem.

Sometimes just describing the situation is enough to solve the problem. Peter might decide to feed the dog when he realizes the situation. Carol might put away the peanut butter and jelly—especially if she's going to want an ant-free sandwich tomorrow. Rory might not want to be late to the rehearsal since he's the soloist.

Use an *I* statement to describe your feelings. The second step in expressing yourself is to use an *I* statement. An *I* statement is one that starts with the words *I feel* and continues from there. This is a way of owning, or taking responsibility for, your feelings. The alternative is to blame the other person with a *you* statement. *You* statements are statements of beliefs, thoughts, or judgments that displace the responsibility for your feelings onto the other person. "You make me so depressed," "You're an ungrateful brat," "You never pay any attention to my needs," are all examples of *you* statements. Notice how blaming and attacking they sound. Recast as *I* statements—"I'm so depressed," "I feel unappreciated," "I feel ignored"—they are less offensive and provocative. These are more mature responses, and they are much more likely to be heard.

You statements can be easily disguised as *I* statements. "*I* feel that *you* are behaving like a spoiled brat" is really a *you* statement in disguise. Phrases such as *I feel like . . .* and *I feel that . . .* are good clues that what follows is likely to be a disguised *you* statement. True *I* statements begin with *I feel* and then continue with a word that describes an emotion, such as happy, sad, depressed, or excited (see the Feelings List in chapter 3 for more examples).

Exercise: Changing You *to* I

Recast these *you* statements as *I* statements.

1. You really make me angry when you say that.

I statement: _____

2. You never think before you act.

I statement: _____

3. You're so thoughtless and unfeeling.

I statement: _____

Example answers:

1. I feel really hurt and offended when you say that.

2. I get really terrified when you do something that I think is dangerous.

3. I feel unappreciated and taken for granted.

Describe what you want or need in the situation. The third step in expressing yourself is to describe what you want or need in the situation. Sometimes this third step is unnecessary. That is, by the time you've described the situation and your feelings about it, the problem is resolved. When that doesn't happen, it's important to be clear about what you want or need in the situation: "I would like you to feed the dog when you get home from school." "I want you to put the food away after you use it." "I'd like to leave as soon as possible." All these are statements that clearly express what the speaker wants.

★ *Carey and Sean* ★

In the original story Carey had never actually expressed herself to Sean. She'd threatened and blamed, but Sean had long since learned to tune that out. So Carey decided to carefully script what she wanted to say to Sean and try it out. The following afternoon she started. "Sean, your coat and shoes are on the kitchen floor [description]. I feel really frustrated when I'm preparing dinner and I have to step over them every time I want to get something out of the fridge [*I* statement]. At the same time, I feel exploited and resentful when I think that you expect me to put them away for you [*I* statement]." To Carey's surprise, Sean picked up his coat and shoes with a brief "Sorry," and disappeared with them upstairs to his room. Carey didn't have to explicitly tell Sean what she wanted. He understood and complied.

✳ *Maddy and Erin* ✳

Maddy realized that she needed to say something to Erin before she got too frustrated or angry. She used the next couple of days when she was off work to prepare exactly what to say. Then she waited until the next time she and Jamie arrived home to the chaos of an unset table and a not-quite-finished dinner. Maddy set the table while Erin finished dinner, and then the three of them sat down to eat. After chatting for a few minutes, Maddy took a deep breath and began. "Erin, I know you're really enjoying your friendship with Shane at the bookstore. I've also noticed that your hanging out with him is interfering with dinner getting prepared on time [description]. When I'm hungry and tired after a really long day and dinner isn't ready, I feel disappointed and frustrated [*I* statement]. I'd like you to be home by five o'clock at the latest so that you'll have an opportunity to finish dinner by the time I get home with Jamie [description of wants or needs]."

To Maddy's relief, Erin (who had feared worse repercussions) said simply, "No problem, I'm sorry I've been flaky recently."

Dos in Expressing Yourself

self-steering wheel

It's important to strive for the following goals when expressing yourself.

Be clear. It's essential to be clear about your thoughts, feelings, wants, and needs without leaving anything out or beating around the bush. It's also important to differentiate between your thoughts, feelings, wants, and needs. When a mother says to her son, "I feel like this is a big mistake and you're heading into trouble again," she's confusing her thoughts—"I *think* this is a big mistake"—with her feelings. Her statement might be more clearly and accurately rephrased like this: "I *think* doing this is a mistake. I *feel* scared and helpless. I *need* you to explain again why you think it's important that you do this."

Lying, however well intentioned, keeps you cut off from others and unable to clearly express yourself.

Some people are afraid to say what they really mean, and therefore they either drop hints or talk in vague, abstract terms. "I want you to set the table for dinner and help clear the dishes away afterwards" is much clearer than "I want you to help out more." "I'd like you to bring me a glass of water when you pour one for yourself" is less vague than "I'm so thirsty I could die."

Be honest. Being honest means stating your true feelings and needs without fear of upsetting the other person. For example, when you're feeling exhausted and want some time to rest, you don't say that you'd really like to help out with your child's homework but you have too much cleaning to do.

Likewise, you don't say that helping out at your child's school went "just fine" when actually you felt criticized the whole time. And you don't say that you're feeling a little sick and need your daughter to stay home and watch the younger children when actually you're feeling anxious about the party she was going to attend.

Lying, however well intentioned, keeps you cut off from others and unable to clearly express yourself.

Be consistent. Especially when talking to children, it's important that what you say and the way you say it don't give two different messages. Your posture, tone of voice, gestures, and so on should match the content of what you're saying. When someone casually asks "How are things?" the typical response is "Fine." Yet many different meanings can be conveyed in that single word with different tones of voice, expressions, and gestures. If things really are fine, your cheerful, positive tone would convey that message. But compare these other messages, conveyed in the same two-word response:

You could say in a sarcastic tone, "*I'm* fine," implying "but *you're* not OK at all."

You could say in a martyred tone, "[*sigh*] I'm fine," implying "actually I'm not well at all, but I'm not worth worrying about."

You could say with frustration, "I'm *fine!*" implying "and I'm feeling really bugged by your constant asking."

Or you could say flippantly, "I'm fine!" implying either "don't take me too seriously" or "I don't really want you to know how I am."

Sometimes inconsistencies, or incongruities, between verbal and nonverbal messages indicate that you don't really know how you feel. Maybe you aren't consciously aware of how frustrated, angry, or resentful you are. If you find yourself giving contradictory messages, you may need to take time out to determine how you actually feel, and then practice conforming your gestures, tone of voice, and posture to fit that feeling, before discussing the issue with your child.

Be appropriate. The expression of your feelings needs to match the strength of those feelings. This is similar to the preceding point about consistency. When you're really angry, say so. Don't say you're "a little frustrated." When you're feeling deeply hurt and disappointed, don't say that you're "a little upset." On the other hand, you don't want to say you're "totally devastated" when you're disappointed that your son got a B on his report card. Don't say that you're "enraged" when you're frustrated that your daughter is ten minutes late. Appropriateness refers to nonverbal communication as well: your tone of voice, posture, gestures. Violent behaviors are never appropriate, for example, screaming, hitting, throwing things. The value of finding the appropriate expression of your feelings is that the risk of acting out those feelings is greatly reduced.

Be immediate. When you have a feeling that needs to be expressed, don't wait until tomorrow or next week. Even waiting an hour diminishes the value of your feedback. This is especially true with children. Young children have very limited memories and are very present oriented. Therefore, they probably won't remember what happened last week, even if it was important to you, unless it was also particularly significant to them. Furthermore, children learn by association. This means that they learn best things that are closely associated in time. For example, suppose your four-year-old behaves badly at a social event and you say nothing, waiting until a "more appropriate" time. Then the next day, when she's coloring, you remind her of the event and tell her how upset you were. Because of the delay, your words probably won't have much meaning to your child. In fact, she is more likely to associate the bad feelings that result from your words to her coloring than to yesterday's event.

When the behavior is recurrent, you can plan a response and wait for the behavior to reappear. But when it occurs (again), you need to say your piece immediately—especially with young children.

Saying right away what you feel in response to a behavior gives your child the opportunity to immediately adjust his or her behavior accordingly. Not expressing your feelings may just cause them to smolder and grow. They may then come out later in an unprovoked explosion or in subtle, passive-aggressive ways. (*Passive-aggressive* refers to behaviors that are not overtly aggressive but are experienced as punishing. Not responding when you're spoken to, dawdling so that appointments are missed, agreeing to do something but then "forgetting," are all examples of passive-aggressive behavior.) Either way the relationship will lose.

Be supportive. Remember that your intention in expressing yourself is to be heard and understood, not to get even or prove yourself right. This means trying to express your feelings honestly without being deliberately hurtful. Say your son is almost an hour late for curfew, and you've gone from being irritated that he's late again to being terrified that something's happened to him. When he finally turns up, you feel tremendous relief that he's alive—followed closely by tremendous anger that you were so worried for so long. Being supportive means expressing the relief ("I'm so glad you're OK. I was scared that something awful had happened to you.") as well as the anger ("It's upsetting to me that you didn't call."), rather than just blowing your stack ("You're so damned thoughtless and irresponsible! You're grounded for a month"). Setting appropriate consequences, as discussed in chapter 7, is a more effective means of deterring negative behaviors than losing your temper.

In simple ways, being supportive means phrasing the things you say in the least hurtful way. "I don't think this is going to work" is more supportive than "That's a stupid plan." "I'd prefer to cook it myself" is more supportive than "Your cooking stinks." "This isn't quite my taste in clothes" is more supportive than "You have lousy taste."

Children are people, too. They don't like being ordered around any more than anyone else does.

Don'ts in Expressing Yourself

The following are things to avoid when talking to your child.

Judge. Judgmental *you* statements accuse and attack your child. They contain "you're bad" messages. Furthermore, they interfere with the accurate expression of your own thoughts, feelings, and needs.

Label. It is OK not to like your child's behavior. It's OK to think the behavior irresponsible, mean, or selfish. However, a statement such as "You're so stupid and irresponsible" is a condemnation of the child him- or herself, rather than of the behavior. Global labels, such as lazy, stupid, arrogant, selfish, worthless, irresponsible, are far more hurtful and damaging than an expression of your dislike for a particular behavior.

Lecture and moralize. No one likes to be told they're wrong. Getting lectured about why you're wrong or why you should be doing things differently just makes it worse. Most children rapidly learn to tune out when they hear a lecture beginning.

Command. Unless you're in the military, chances are that it doesn't sit well when someone orders you to do something. Commands imply a lack of equality and respect in a relationship, and in many people they trigger an automatic refusal to comply. Children are people, too. They don't like being ordered around any more than anyone else does. If you want to foster a relationship of mutual respect and understanding, it's important to use the courteous gestures and phrases that in our society communicate respect. "Could you please pass the water?" is more respectful than "Get me the water."

Threaten. Once again, it's important to keep in mind that your intention in expressing yourself is to increase the level of understanding in your relationship with your child. You cannot accomplish this by threatening. Threats serve no purpose other than to intimidate your child into behaving the way you want him or her to. The more fear there is in a relationship, the less room there is for respect and caring. Threats can also lead to the child adopting the same sort of behavior with others.

Make negative comparisons. Negative comparisons not only contain "you're bad" messages, they also make your child feel inferior to others. "Why can't you take care of your possessions like Damon does?" "Sarah is always willing to help her mother do the shopping. Why aren't you?" "Why can't you be more like your brother—he's much more cooperative and nice to be around."

These are all examples of negative comparisons. Negative comparisons arouse feelings of defensiveness, rather than a desire to understand your feelings and needs and to improve the relationship.

Whatever you say or do, you are expressing yourself. However, it's clear that there are ways of expressing yourself that are more likely both to be heard and to engage the cooperation of your child. When you judge, label, threaten, or lecture your child, you are likely to stir up feelings of defensiveness. But when you describe your feelings about the situation using an *I* statement, and when you're clear, honest, and supportive, you contribute to the building of a strong and meaningful relationship.

Keys to Expressing Yourself

★ Describe the situation.

★ Use an *I* statement to describe your feelings.

★ Describe what you want or need in the situation.

5

How to Determine Whose Problem It Is

It's probably clear to you by now that a variety of skills are involved in having a satisfying relationship—whether it is with a child, parent, lover, friend, or anyone else. In particular, you've learned the skills of listening and expressing yourself. It may, however, be less clear when to apply each of these skills. This chapter will explore the ideas that the appropriate response depends on who "owns" the problem and that who owns the problem depends on whose rights are being affected. By the end of this chapter, you will be able to determine who owns the problem in a wide variety of situations.

A Question of Rights

When someone you know and care about—your child, parent, friend, colleague, or lover—is having a problem, your major role is to listen (see chapter 3). *Active listening* describes the process of helping another person feel heard and understood. Although useful in virtually every situation, its best application is when someone is having a problem.

When people have a problem, it usually means that they are either having difficulty getting their needs met or their rights are being violated in some way. Unfortunately, for most people this is a normal daily occurrence. A person's needs can be thwarted every day in countless ways. The best indicator that someone is having a problem is when he or she begins to express negative feelings.

The use of active listening at these times helps the other person know that the problem—and his or her feelings and concerns about the problem—have been heard and understood. It also communicates some important messages: that you care about the person, that you respect his or her feelings, and that you assume this person has at least some of the resources necessary to solve the problem.

What about when you have a problem? When the problem is yours, you need to use your skills at expressing yourself, starting with an *I* statement (see chapter 4). An *I* statement requires a nonblaming account of your feelings and needs with respect to a particular problem you're having.

So sometimes it's appropriate to use active listening and sometimes *I* statements, depending on who is encountering the problem. But in some situations it's unclear who's having the problem and therefore which response to use. The question of who "owns" the problem is linked to the question of whose needs are not being met or whose rights are being affected.

As human beings, everyone has certain rights. Unfortunately, worldwide there is little agreement about what those rights are. The United States' Bill of

Rights is supposed to guarantee certain civil rights, such as the right to free speech, the right to a fair and speedy trial, and the right to be protected from unlawful search and seizure. On a less grand, more everyday level, you and everyone else have basic human rights as well, for example, the right to live and to think and believe as you choose to.

Most of your actions are probably based on assumptions about the existence of certain rights—even if you have not consciously defined for yourself what they are. Your list of rights may resemble those assembled by psychologist Manuel J. Smith in his "Bill of Assertive Rights." His list includes the following:

* The right to be the ultimate judge of your own behavior, feelings, and thoughts

* The right to change your mind

* The right to make mistakes (and be responsible for them)

* The right to say "I don't know," "I don't understand," and "No" (without feeling guilty)

* The right to not take responsibility for finding solutions to other people's problems

Notice that none of these rights involves controlling or manipulating the behavior of others.

Exercise: Identifying Your Rights

In the space provided below, write some other rights that you have, for example, "I have the right to be treated respectfully" or "I have the right to expect my possessions to be treated carefully when someone borrows them."

I have the right to _____

I have the right to _____

I have the right to _____

Who Owns the Problem?

As a parent, you have four possible answers to the question "Who owns the problem?"

- You own the problem.
- Your child owns the problem.
- You both own the problem.
- There is no problem.

When your daughter tells you about the disappointment she's experiencing with her new boyfriend, is that your problem or hers? It's unlikely that your needs or rights are involved in your daughter's relationship problems. If your three-year-old tells you that he got a time-out at preschool for hitting another child, is that your problem or his? Here, too, your child has already experienced the consequences of his behavior and at this point your needs and rights probably aren't involved.

On the other hand, what if your ten-year-old borrows your portable CD player and loses it? Or your two-year-old gets into your makeup cabinet and empties your expensive perfume down the sink? Or your sixteen-year-old borrows your car and returns it with an empty gas tank and a dented fender? In these examples, your needs and rights are very definitely involved.

Sorting out whose problem it is ranges from easy to difficult, depending on the complexity of the situation. The following are some rules of thumb:

Your child owns the problem when his or her needs or rights are being thwarted, not yours. You may not like what's happening, but if it's not interfering with your rights, it's not your problem. Although he or she may talk to you about it, dealing with the problem or finding a solution is his or her responsibility.

Controlling another's behavior is not a right.

You own the problem when your child is satisfying his or her needs but his or her behavior is interfering with your rights or your needs. When the problem is yours the responsibility for solving the problem is yours as well.

You both own the problem when your child has a problem because his or her needs are being thwarted, but his or her reactions to the problem or attempts to solve the problem are interfering with your needs or rights.

There is no problem when your child is satisfying his or her needs and his or her behavior isn't interfering with your rights in any way.

Exercise: Whose Problem?

In each of the following situations, determine who owns the problem and check the corresponding box. Is it your problem or your child's? If your child's problem is creating a problem for you, so that you both have a problem, check both boxes. If neither of you has a problem—that is, there is no problem—leave both boxes blank.

	Your Problem	*Your Child's Problem*
1. Your son tells you that he's upset because his boss is cutting his hours.	☐	☐
2. Your preschool daughter tells you how sad she is because her friend said she doesn't want to play with her anymore.	☐	☐
3. Your son told some friends of his confidential information you had told him.	☐	☐
4. Your ten-year-old isn't doing her chores around the house.	☐	☐
5. Your sixteen-year-old is driving somewhat carelessly—with you in the car.	☐	☐
6. Your seven-year-old fought with his best friend for the second day in a row.	☐	☐
7. Your two-year-old keeps interrupting you while you're on the telephone.	☐	☐
8. Your four-year-old wants to take his toys to bed with him.	☐	☐
9. Your fifteen-year-old wants to get his hair cut in a style that you really dislike.	☐	☐
10. Your daughter at boarding school keeps telling you that she's going to write—and then doesn't.	☐	☐

Answers:

1. Your son is upset; his needs for work hours (money) are not being satisfied. However, your needs are not affected. Thus the problem is your child's, not yours.

2. Your preschool daughter is sad because her friend doesn't want to play with her. Your needs are not affected by the situation. It is your child's problem.

3. When your son told his friends the confidential information you had told him, he was interfering with your right to privacy. Therefore the problem is yours.

4. If your ten-year-old isn't doing her chores around the house, then your right to have your agreements honored is being thwarted. You own the problem.

5. If your sixteen-year-old is driving carelessly with you in the car then she is interfering with your need to feel safe. You own the problem. However, if your concerns about her driving are serious enough to restrict her use of the car, then she also has a problem. You both own the problem.

6. As long as your seven-year-old's safety isn't at risk, his fights with his friend aren't interfering with your needs or rights.

To develop into separate individuals with their own identities—to become autonomous and independent—children must be allowed to explore what they *think, feel, want, and believe.*

The problem is his. However, if his or his friend's safety is at risk, then you also own the problem.

7. When your two-year-old continually interrupts your phone conversation, it's your needs that are being thwarted. You own the problem.

8. Your four-year-old wants to take his toys to bed with him. It's unlikely that your rights would be affected by that behavior. However, if the toys he wants to take to bed are dirty or wet, could tear the sheets, or might otherwise cause damage then your rights are being affected and the problem is both yours and your son's, whose needs aren't being allowed.

9. Your fifteen-year-old wants to get his hair cut in a style you dislike. Again, unless your son's behavior has some direct negative impact on your needs (other than the desire to control his behavior, which isn't a true need) there shouldn't be a problem here. Of course, your son may experience problems as a result of his decision, but they would be his problems.

10. When your daughter doesn't follow through with the behavior she's promised, it's your needs that are being thwarted—the need to be able to trust your child. Thus you own the problem.

Letting Go of Your Child's Problems

Even when you can see that a problem really isn't your responsibility, it can be hard to let go. For example, if you feel very strongly that an education is the only route to success, it can be hard to listen to your teenager express his discouragement at school and his thoughts about dropping out. It can be difficult to accept that this is his problem, not yours, and that it's not your responsibility to talk him into graduating. Though if he asks your opinion it doesn't mean you must refrain from giving one.

It's hard enough to let go of a problem that really belongs to a friend, lover, or parent. It's even harder to let go when the problem belongs to your child. Partly out of a desire to protect their children, most parents want some measure of control over their children's lives, and they try to mold their children into conforming to their own beliefs and needs. However, to develop into separate individuals with their own identities—to become autonomous and independent—children must be allowed to explore what *they* think, feel, want, and believe. They must be allowed to make their own decisions and deal with their own problems their own way—provided that their health and safety aren't at risk. Often children express their separateness by flaunting differences in those areas most dear to their parents: appearance, language, political opinions. Although some parents may experience the expression of these differences as *their* problem, in these situations usually either the problem is the child's or there is no problem.

Taking over your child's problems not only denies him or her the experience of solving them independently, it also says that you don't believe that your child is capable of solving his or her own problems. Moreover, fighting over things that ultimately aren't your responsibility not only makes your life more difficult, but it may jeopardize your relationship with your child.

✳ *Jerry's Story* ✳

Eight-year-old Jerry was telling his father about a fight he'd had with his best friend, Rick. Jerry was hurt and angry and wanted nothing more to do with Rick. It wasn't Jerry's father's problem, nor was it his responsibility to tell Jerry how to fix things with his friend. However, his father believed that forgiveness is the best policy, and he tried to convince Jerry of that. The ensuing argument left Jerry feeling discouraged and angry with his father and their relationship a little shaky.

★ *Maria's Story* ★

Maria had just turned twelve when she decided that she wanted to wear makeup when she went out with her friends. She had saved up her allowance and planned to buy a small kit. Her mother was adamantly opposed to the idea. Her opposition was based less on a concern for Maria's health or safety—which she agreed probably weren't at risk—than what she felt was "appropriate." Maria tried to argue that it wasn't her mother's problem—that her mother's rights really weren't involved, since the right to control another's behavior isn't a legitimate right. But it was no use: Her mother forbade Maria to wear makeup.

However, because she was taking responsibility for something that wasn't really her problem, Maria's mother discovered that it was impossible to enforce her preference. Instead, she realized that she was inadvertently encouraging Maria to be sneaky, to wait till she got out of the house before putting on makeup. She also realized that she had risked her relationship with her daughter to try to enforce a solution to a problem that not only wasn't hers but that didn't actually exist. Pushing your solutions onto someone else's problem just doesn't work.

✴ *Carolyn's Story* ✴

Carolyn's daughter, Angel, was sixteen. They had lived alone since Carolyn's husband died twelve years before. For the most part they got along easily: They shared household chores, were both fairly neat, and respected the other's privacy. Then Angel broke up with her boyfriend. At first Carolyn was able to empathize with her daughter's unhappiness—she could see how miserable Angel was. When Angel seemed to be constantly in a bad mood, Carolyn didn't take it personally. She knew Angel was having a problem dealing with the breakup. But when their house began looking, and smelling, like a dump—partly because Angel couldn't summon the energy to clean up after herself and partly because periodically she flew into rages and threw things around—Carolyn realized that she also had a problem.

Angel had a right to her feelings, to her disappointment and unhappiness, and a right to express those feelings. However, the way she was expressing her feelings was interfering with Carolyn's rights to have a reasonably clean house and possessions that would not be broken. Angel's breakup was her responsibility, but Carolyn also had a problem and it was her responsibility to deal with it and find a solution.

✴ *Janet's Story* ✴

Corey, at five, was developing his drawing skills with crayons and marking pens. He loved drawing and would scribble on anything he could get his hands on. He was also beginning to recognize the limitations of his skill, that his drawings didn't look the way he wanted them to. Despite reassurances from his mother, Janet, that his skills would improve as he got older, Corey had episodes of intense frustration. Janet tolerated the frustration because she realized that it had nothing to do with her—it was Corey's problem.

One day Corey's frustration was so powerful that he gathered all his crayons, threw them on the floor, and stomped on them—right on the newly cleaned carpets. At this point, Janet also had a problem. Corey's manifestation of frustration was interfering with Janet's right not to have her carpets unnecessarily ruined. Like Carolyn, Janet had a problem in addition to her child's, and it was her responsibility to find a solution for it.

Knowing who owns the problem is essential in determining how to respond to that particular situation. Deciding whose rights are being violated is the key to the puzzle.

When you own the problem, you have the responsibility for trying to solve it. That means engaging the skills of expressing yourself described in the previous chapter. It may also involve using problem-solving skills (described in chapter 6) or setting appropriate consequences (see chapter 7).

On the other hand, when the problem isn't yours but your child's, then your responsibilities are quite different. In those circumstances, your responsibility is to listen and be supportive, to provide the best possible environment for your child to try to solve his or her problem.

Sometimes ownership of the problem is unclear. Perhaps both your rights and those of your child are being violated. Or perhaps your child's response to a problem is leading to a violation of your rights. In each of these cases, both you and your child own the problem. Each of you then has a responsibility to try to solve your own problem.

And sometimes, when you can determine that your own needs and rights are not affected, then it's clear that there is no problem.

Keys to Determining Whose Problem It Is

★ Your child's problem: Your child's needs or rights are being thwarted, not yours.

★ Your problem: Your needs or rights are being thwarted.

★ A joint problem: Your child's needs or rights are being thwarted, and his or her reactions to the problem or attempts to solve the problem are interfering with your needs or rights.

★ No problem: Your child is satisfying his or her needs and his or her behavior isn't interfering with your rights in any way.

6

How to Solve Problems

No two people have exactly the same needs. Therefore, whenever people get together conflicts of need inevitably occur. This is true whether the people involved are parent and child, teacher and student, lovers, or friends. It is often tempting to think that your own needs are more important or more "right," especially when the other person is your child. However, the fact that two people have different needs doesn't mean that one person is right and the other is wrong. Both people's needs are valid, and any solution to the problem of these different needs must take both you and your child into account. In this chapter you'll learn the six-step approach used to solve the problem of conflicting needs.

✸ *Tamra and Marty's Story* ✸

Marty, at almost four, had very definite ideas about things. One of those things was brushing his teeth. The dentist had made it clear to Marty's mother, Tamra, that she needed to help Marty brush his teeth. To Tamra, that meant brushing them for him. She didn't want to risk his getting cavities, because of the upset as well as the cost. Marty, on the other hand, had his own ideas about who, how, and when his teeth should be brushed—and they didn't include his mother at all! His preference was a short, sweet chew on the toothbrush (just enough to remove the yummy toothpaste), when he felt like it, and definitely without any help from anyone else. There were endless battles at bedtime, with Marty refusing to open his mouth for a proper cleaning and Tamra making various threats about no bedtime stories or TV the next day. Marty often went to bed in tears, with Tamra not far from tears herself.

> *The fact that two people have different needs doesn't mean that one person is right and the other is wrong.*

✸ *Jim and Renee's Story* ✸

Jim had had many discussions with friends and other parents about pets before deciding to buy two goldfish for his six-year-old daughter, Renee. Jim had been reluctant to buy any kind of pet, because he didn't want the responsibility of taking care of it to end up being his. He was busy enough coping as a single father. But Renee begged and begged for a pet, vowing to do whatever was necessary for its care. Renee seemed like a pretty responsible kid, so finally Jim relented. Renee was absolutely delighted with her two fish, which she immediately named Goldie Fish and Goldie Brown.

Initially, Renee took her responsibility of feeding the fish each morning very seriously. She would get up before her father had awakened, and after giving the fish their food, would sit in front of the tank and watch them eat, providing a running commentary—to the fish—on their behavior. Eventually, however, she fell back into her morning routine of turning on the TV until her father got up. Goldie Fish and Goldie Brown went hungry.

Any solution to the problem of different needs must take both you and your child into account.

When he remembered, Jim would ask Renee if she'd fed the fish, and often she would leap from the couch apologetically and feed them then. At other times, she would absently answer, "Yes," but her lack of conviction wasn't completely reassuring to Jim. Most frustrating were the times when at dinner Renee would suddenly exclaim, "Oh no! The fish!" and rush off to feed them. Jim could see the writing on the wall, and he decided that something had to change.

Six Steps to Problem Solving

In both of the preceding situations there are two people with very different needs. Neither of them is wrong—none of the needs are bad. These are simply examples of the inevitable conflict that any two people experience over time. The important question is: How can the problems be solved?

The following six steps to problem solving are adapted from *When Anger Hurts Your Kids*, by Matthew McKay et al.:

1. Talk about your child's feelings and needs.

2. Talk about your own feelings and needs.

3. Brainstorm all possible solutions without judgment.

4. Eliminate those solutions that are not mutually agreeable.

5. Pick the best solution or combination of alternatives.

6. Develop a plan for implementation and evaluation.

Step 1: Talk about your child's feelings and needs. This is possibly the most important step of the entire process. Unless you really understand what your child wants and needs, you won't be able to find a solution that takes those needs into account. Furthermore, unless your child believes that you really are interested in understanding his or her feelings and needs—and knows that you're not just giving lip service to the "joint" aspect of problem solving—then you'll be wasting your time. Don't assume you know. Ask for clarification. And above all, don't use statements that attribute blame to your child for having needs which differ from yours.

✳ *Tamra and Marty*

The problem between Marty and his mother wasn't that Tamra was mean, nor that Marty was irresponsible. Their problem was that Marty wanted to flex his independence and brush his teeth all by himself, while Tamra wanted to ensure that his teeth were really clean by brushing them herself. Let's say Tamra decided to take a problem-solving approach to the problem. Step 1 in the process might have sounded like this:

Tamra: Marty, I understand that you think you're big enough to brush your teeth alone, and would like to do it without my help. Is that right?

Marty: Yes!

✳ *Jim and Renee*

Similarly, Jim and Renee's problem wasn't that Renee was too immature and irresponsible, nor that Jim was uptight. Their problem was that Jim didn't want to have to be responsible for the care of the fish, and that Renee really wanted the fish but seemed to have trouble remembering to feed them. Their Step 1 interaction might have sounded like this:

Jim: Renee, I've noticed that the fish missed their morning feed four times this week. I know you love the fish and want them to get the care they need. Do you see this as a problem?

Renee: Yes! I want to remember but I just forget!

Step 2: Talk about your own feelings and needs. Keep the description of your needs brief. Don't try to convince your child that your feelings and needs are more important than his or hers. Use this opportunity to convey the message that both of you have feelings and needs that are valid.

☆ *Tamra and Marty* ☆

Tamra and Marty's interaction might have continued this way:

Tamra: Marty, I worry that if you don't get your teeth really clean you'll get cavities, and that will hurt as well as cost money that I'd rather not have to spend.

☆ *Jim and Renee* ☆

Jim and Renee's interaction might have continued this way:

Jim: Renee, I feel really bad for the fish. Often they only get fed because I remind you, and I worry that if I didn't remind you they might not get fed at all. And the thing is, I don't want to have to remind you. I have enough to remember of my own.

Step 3: Brainstorm all possible solutions without judgment. Once you've clarified each person's feelings and needs, you can begin brainstorming possible solutions. It helps to write down all the suggestions so that they're not forgotten from one step to the next. If possible, let your child come up with the first couple of suggestions. It's important not to judge or criticize any suggestion, no matter how impractical or impossible you think it is. In fact, a few way-out suggestions may introduce a bit of humor into what may otherwise feel like a very serious process. The more potential solutions you can think of, the better your chances of finding one that at least partially meets both your needs.

Tamra and Marty

Tamra and Marty might have continued their problem-solving interaction in this way:

Tamra: What can we do about this? Let's brainstorm. I'll write down our suggestions. What do you think?

Marty (laughing): I brush my teeth by myself!

Tamra: OK, I'll write that down. What else? I guess I should write down the possibility that you let me brush them for you.

Marty: What about I brush them first and then you check them . . .

Tamra: Kind of do a tidy-up job? OK. Hmmm. What else? . . . You could always brush your own teeth but stop eating desserts and candy so that you're less likely to get cavities.

Marty: Yuck!

Jim and Renee

Jim and Renee might have continued their problem-solving interaction like this:

Jim: Let's brainstorm some solutions— I'll write them down. Let's not decide if they're any good, just list them. One suggestion is that we take the fish back to the store until you're older.

Renee: You could just feed the fish for me! Well, at least keep reminding me to feed them. No, I know you don't want either of those.

Jim: It's OK, I'll write them down. What if you were to make yourself some kind of reminder to feed them? A sign or a picture or something?

Renee: Yeah, or what if I put a lot of food in the tank every few days and then didn't have to worry about remembering in between?

You want to consider only those suggestions that both of you can live with.

Step 4: Eliminate those solutions that are not mutually agreeable. The fourth step in problem solving is to review your list of suggestions and eliminate those that *either* of you finds unacceptable. Since you're looking for compromise, you want to consider only those suggestions that both of you can live with. Read aloud each item on your list. If you think one wouldn't work, say so *without criticism.* "I don't think that would work for me" is better than "That's a stupid suggestion." Remember, if one of you wants to eliminate a suggestion, then it needs to be crossed off. Justifications are not necessary.

Take this opportunity to explain why you think something might be a good alternative and worth keeping. Your partner in problem-solving might not have considered that. If however, despite your persuasiveness, he or she still wants to eliminate that alternative, it gets eliminated.

At the end of this step, you should have at least one possible solution that would work for both of you. If not—if all the items have been eliminated—you have two options: You can brainstorm more alternatives, or you can reconsider some of the solutions you crossed off your list.

✳ *Tamra and Marty* ✳

Tamra and Marty might have continued in this way:

Tamra: If neither of us has any more suggestions, let's go through our list and evaluate. I'll read out each suggestion, and if one of us doesn't want it, I'll cross it out. The first one is that you brush your teeth on your own. I'm not willing to keep that one because the dentist says your teeth won't get clean enough. *(She crosses it off the list.)* The next one is you let me brush them for you.

Marty: No! I hate that one!

Tamra: OK, I'll cross it off. The next suggestion is that you brush your teeth first and I do a cleanup afterwards. That would be OK with me. What about you?

Marty: Yeah, that's OK.

Tamra: Lastly, you do it yourself but stop eating desserts and candy to reduce the chances of cavities.

Marty: No! I hate that one, too!

✳ *Jim and Renee* ✳

Jim and Renee might have continued like this:

Jim: OK, so let me read out the suggestions. The first one is that I feed the fish for you. I'm afraid I'm not willing to do that. *(He crosses it off the list.)* The next suggestion is that I keep reminding you to feed them. I don't want to do that either.

Renee: ·I knew you wouldn't! You shouldn't have bothered writing them down.

Jim: Well, I think it's important to write down everything we come up with during the brainstorming, even if we kind of know that they're not going to work. Now, what's next . . . You make some kind of sign or picture to remind yourself to feed them. That's OK with me.

Renee: That's OK with me, too.

Jim: Lastly, you give the fish a lot of food every few days and then don't have to worry about remembering. I'm not happy with that one. Fish can die from overeating. And besides, how would you like it if I made a big bowl of pasta and then left it sitting out for you for a few days so I didn't have to worry about cooking?

Renee: Yuck! OK, cross that off.

Step 5:   Pick the best solution or combination of alternatives. The fifth step in problem solving is to pick the best solution or combination of solutions from the remaining options on your list. You need to have at least one mutually agreeable solution left on your list before progressing to this step. If a variety of options remain, decide together which one you want to try.

✳ *Tamra and Marty* ✳

Since only one option is left on their list, this step would be easy for Tamra and Marty:

Tamra: Well, the suggestion that we both thought was OK is that you brush your teeth first and I do a cleanup afterwards. Shall we try that?

Marty: OK.

✳ *Jim and Renee* ✳

Only one option is left on Jim and Renee's list, so their next step would also be easy:

Jim: The only suggestion that we both thought was OK is for you to make some kind of sign or picture to remind yourself to feed the fish. Shall we try that one?

Renee: OK.

Step 6: Develop a plan for implementation and evaluation. First think through the details of how you will put the new plan to work. Then decide how long you want to try it before evaluating its success. It's useful to develop a fallback plan in case the first solution doesn't work. Sometimes this plan may be one of the other alternatives on your list (the second-best choice). At other times it might involve consequences designed by either you alone or in consultation with your child (see chapter 7).

✳ *Tamra and Marty*

Tamra: So, when should we begin this plan?

Marty: Tonight?

Tamra: Sounds good to me. And how about we try it for a week and see how it works?

Marty: OK.

Tamra: Now. What if it doesn't work? What if you won't let me do the cleanup?

Marty: I will, I will. I promise!

Tamra: I know you want to, sweetie, but I think we should have a backup plan just in case. For example, if you don't let me do the cleanup one day, then the next day you won't eat any dessert or candy—something like that. But we'll try the plan for a week without consequences first. What do you think?

Marty (reluctantly): All right. But I will let you do the cleanup!

Tamra: Great!

✳ *Jim and Renee*

Renee: How about I go get my markers and make up a sign right now? And I could put it right by my bed so I see it every morning!

Jim: That's a great idea. When should we decide if it's working or not?

Renee: We'll be able to tell right away. But how about we decide officially next week?

Jim: OK. And if it isn't working?

Renee: I guess that would mean you'd want to take them back to the store wouldn't it? *(Jim nods)* I'll just make sure that that doesn't have to happen!

For almost every problem that arises between you and your child, the six steps described above can be used to develop a satisfactory solution. As long as you're clear about defining and validating the feelings and needs each of you has, you'll be able to brainstorm a list of possible solutions that directly address that problem. Eliminating the options that are unacceptable to either of you is necessary to assure that you come up with at least one alternative that is indeed a valid and potential solution. Developing a detailed plan will ensure that the chosen option is given the best possible chance of success.

A modified version of this strategy can be used even with very small children. As soon as children are able to articulate their wants and needs, they can engage in problem solving. In fact, they are often able to come up with creative and successful solutions to the conflict.

Effective parenting is rooted in respect for your child. Any attempt at problem solving that communicates respect for your child's feelings, needs, and ideas will enhance your relationship while reducing misbehavior.

Keys to Problem Solving

★ Talk about your child's feelings and needs.

★ Talk about your own feelings and needs.

★ Brainstorm all possible solutions without judgment.

★ Eliminate those solutions that are not mutually agreeable.

★ Pick the best solution or combination of alternatives.

★ Develop a plan for implementation and evaluation.

7

How to Design Choices and Consequences

If you are like most people, you probably grew up in a family where misbehavior was soundly punished. You were probably told—or even ordered—to do things without being given much choice about how, when, or whether you did those things.

In this chapter you'll learn why punishment is not the best response to misbehavior. You'll learn how being offered choices builds self-esteem in children. You'll also learn how letting children experience the consequences of their behavior—the events that result from the choices they make—builds their sense of responsibility. The difference between natural and logical consequences will be discussed. Lastly, time out as a choice or consequence will be discussed.

✶ *Carey and Janey's Story* ✶

Three-year-old Carey loved waking up on Easter morning to find that the Easter bunny had come while she was sleeping. A brief hunt netted her some decorated hard-boiled eggs as well as some chocolate eggs. She was allowed to eat two of her chocolate eggs after breakfast, with the promise of two more after lunch and two more after dinner. The hard-boiled eggs were put in the fridge to be made into egg salad. The remaining chocolate eggs were left in a bowl on the table.

Later that morning, Carey's mom, Janey, realized that she couldn't hear Carey playing anymore and that she hadn't for several minutes. She headed up the hallway to Carey's room and found the door closed and locked. She could have opened the lock herself with a coin, but instead Janey knocked and asked Carey to open the door. Carey mumbled something in response that was barely intelligible. It sounded to Janey like Carey had something in her mouth. Chocolate?

When Carey finally opened the door, Janey's suspicions were confirmed. The telltale signs were there: bits of colored-foil wrapping scattered on the floor, brown smudges around Carey's mouth, and the strong smell of chocolate. Carey initially denied having taken and eaten any of the chocolate eggs, but eventually she acknowledged eating two of them and pointed to where the rest of the uneaten eggs were hidden.

Exercise: Disciplining Carey

If you were Janey, which of the following responses would you choose? Check one or more of the options.

☐   Tell Carey that she's a bad girl.

☐   Yell at Carey for disobeying you.

☐   Spank Carey for disobeying you.

☐   Take away the rest of the eggs and tell Carey she can't have anymore of them.

☐   Give Carey a time-out for disobeying you.

☐   Throw away the rest of the chocolate eggs—or eat them yourself.

☐   Develop some other punishment.

☐   Tell Carey that since she ate her two after lunch eggs, she couldn't have any more until after dinner. And put the rest of the eggs in a safe, out-of-reach place.

Why Punishment Doesn't Work

All children misbehave. Growing up requires that you test your developing independence, which means pushing limits. It means disobeying rules to see whether they really are firm and going beyond what your parents say is OK to see who's in charge. As a parent, it's your job to maintain appropriate limits. But it's also your job to nurture your child and foster his or her self-esteem. How can you pursue such apparently contradictory goals at the same time? There are two key things to remember: The doer is not the deed, and punishment is not the best deterrent.

Separating the doer from the deed   means letting your child know that you don't like his or her *behavior* without condemning him or her as "bad," "awful," "evil," or "wicked."

Approaching problems from the standpoint of behavior begins to call into question the concept of punishment. If you assume that your role as a parent is to raise a mature, responsible human being, then punishment doesn't work, for a number of reasons:

Punishment almost always involves anger.   This is the most important reason that punishment doesn't work. When you punish your child, you're usually angry. Anger is frightening, especially to a child. So instead of teaching responsibility, you are teaching your child to be afraid of you. For example, every time Joel sensed that his father was getting angry, he dropped what he was doing, ran to his bedroom, and hid under the bed.

Punishment teaches your child to avoid punishment.   Rather than doing what you want him or her to do because it's the right thing, your child may simply try to avoid punishment. So instead of learning how to make better, more responsible decisions, he or she learns how to avoid getting caught.

For instance, when her mother found Maria (from chapter 5) putting on makeup before school one morning, she forbade her to wear it and took it away. Rather than protesting, twelve-year-old Maria simply kept quiet and promptly went out after school and bought some more makeup. Now, however, she waited until she was on the bus to apply it and made sure she removed it before she got home.

Punishment is often illogical. When punishment is unrelated to the misbehavior it doesn't make sense to the child. Without the necessary connection—a cause-and-effect relationship—the child can't understand why his or her behavior was wrong or learn how to make more responsible decisions. He or she just gets confused.

The doer is not the deed, and punishment is not the best deterrent.

For example, five-year-old Karen was getting ready to go to a friend's birthday party. She was dressed in her prettiest dress, and she chattered nonstop as her mother brushed her hair. Karen was so excited that she wriggled and jiggled under her mother's aggravated yanking. She heard her mother hissing repeatedly, "Stand still," and she did try, but it was hard. Suddenly her mother screamed, "Fine! There's no TV for you tonight!" Confused, Karen went silent. She knew her mother didn't like her wriggling, but where did TV come into it?

Punishment often evokes anger. Punishment sometimes makes the child so angry that instead of thinking about how to behave more appropriately, he or she is distracted by revenge fantasies. This happens most frequently when the punishment is out of proportion to the misbehavior—as often happens.

For instance, when Brian returned home from his date twenty minutes after curfew, his father told him that he couldn't use the car again for a month.

Brian spent the rest of the night fantasizing about getting revenge by making a big scratch down the side of his father's car.

Punishment can teach that "might makes right." Physical punishment and other treatment that relies on intimidation—such as anger or threats—teaches that you can get what you want through the use of power and coercion. This may be the opposite of what you're intending to teach and in the long run is unlikely to be a positive tactic for your child to learn. For example, Stuart was playing with his blocks when his little brother came running over and knocked them down. Stuart was furious and began hitting his brother, whose cries quickly brought their mother. She grabbed Stuart and began hitting him, yelling while she did so, "This will teach you to hit your brother . . ." And it did.

Punishment can reinforce the behavior. Sometimes punishment gives much-desired attention that actually reinforces the misbehavior. For instance, Herb was in the garage, cleaning his fishing gear in readiness for his weekend away with friends from work. His four-year-old son, Nick, kept coming up and disturbing his concentration, picking up pieces of Herb's equipment, playing with the delicate flies, asking unnecessary questions and requests. Herb brusquely told Nick to go back in the house and play with his siblings, and he did—for a few minutes. But soon Nick was back again. This time Herb raised his voice at Nick and told him to leave him in peace. Again it worked for a few minutes. Eventually Herb got so frustrated that he slapped a fishing fly out of Nick's hand. When Nick started crying, Herb guiltily stopped his own work to apologize and comfort him. Herb didn't realize that what Nick wanted was just some attention. So the more he scolded, the more attention he was giving Nick, and therefore the more he reinforced Nick's behavior. When

Herb finally put his work aside and gave Nick his full attention, he was rewarding him even more.

Why Choices and Consequences Work

To learn to act responsibly, children need to know that they have choices and that there are consequences to the choices they make. You experience the consequences of the choices you make every day. If you don't take a sweater and the weather turns nasty, you get cold. If you don't get up when your alarm goes off, you have to choose between being late or skipping breakfast—and there are consequences to each of these choices. If you don't go to work, you don't get your paycheck. If you treat your friends badly, they don't want to be your friends anymore. Without these choices, you would never be able to learn how to behave in the best, most responsible ways.

When children are given choices, they learn that they have the power to make decisions for themselves. They learn that they can make good decisions or bad decisions (for example, to misbehave), and that their choices will bring consequences. There are many reasons why giving choices is important. Choices separate the doer from the deed. When you give children choices you imply that they are separate from their behavior, that they are capable of making good decisions as well as bad decisions. You also imply that even if they make bad decisions they aren't bad people for doing so.

When a child really has a choice and makes the decision to act badly, the child may still have a hard time accepting the consequences, but he or she won't feel bad about himself or herself as a person. Moreover, he or she will have learned something from the experience, which makes it less likely that the same choice to misbehave will be made in the future.

When you are giving a choice, remember that the choice should concern (for example) *when* a task is done (Do you want to have your bath before dinner or after?), *how* a task is done (Do you want a bath with or without bubbles?), or *with whom* a task is done (Do you want me or your dad to help with your bath?)—but not *whether* the task is done. In other words, the choice has to be valid, and in this case the child doesn't really have the choice of whether or not to have a bath.

Choices must also be *age appropriate*. It's important to keep in mind the age and developmental skills of your child when you give choices. For example, the choice of whether to walk to school or ride his bike may be appropriate for a ten-year-old, but is not at all appropriate for a five-year-old unless you are going to go along. The choice of getting her own cereal in the morning or wait for you to get up may be appropriate for a four-year-old but not for a two-year-old, who simply wouldn't have the necessary skills to make that a valid choice.

Natural Versus Logical Consequences

It's essential that children learn that their choices have consequences. There are two kinds of consequences: natural and logical. Natural consequences occur without any kind of intervention from you. If eight-year-old Kenny forgets to take his lunch to school, the natural consequence is that he'll be hungry at lunch time. You might think that the best response is to jump in your car and deliver the forgotten lunch. In fact, however, this prevents Kenny from experiencing the consequences of his actions. He doesn't learn how to remember to take his lunch because he doesn't have to learn the lesson offered by the situation. Instead, he learns that if he forgets his lunch someone will always bring it to him. You could nag, threaten, and punish, but if you bring Kenny his lunch, the message that he'll retain is that remembering to take his lunch to school is unnecessary.

If Kenny is healthy, he won't suffer serious harm from missing lunch for a day or two. But the experience of being hungry as a direct result of his own choice—to remember or not to remember—will have a profound learning impact on him.

Logical consequences are those that require your intervention. If Kenny borrows something of yours and loses it at school, chances are that you won't let him borrow anything else of yours to take to school (at least for a while). To withhold your property from someone who doesn't take proper care of it is a logical consequence of that carelessness. It might also be a logical consequence to ask that Kenny replace the lost item out of his allowance money.

These are logical consequences rather than natural consequences because they wouldn't happen on their own. Nothing would automatically happen to Kenny without your intervention. Thus, refusing to lend something next time or requesting replacement of the lost item are logical rather than natural consequences. Always look for a natural consequence first. If there is one, you won't need to intervene, and your child won't see the consequence as originating with you.

Exercise: Logical or Natural?

Look at the following examples and determine whether natural consequences would automatically occur or whether the application of logical consequences is required. The most useful question to ask in completing this exercise is whether anything would automatically happen to the child as a result of his or her behavior. If so, as long as the child is not in danger, then let that natural consequence occur. If not, or if the child would be endangered in some way, then intervene with a logical consequence.

	Natural	Logical
1. Three-year-old Jillie throws sand at the other children at the playground.	☐	☐
2. Four-year-old Tom refuses to take his raincoat when rain is predicted.	☐	☐
3. Two-year-old Rebeccah constantly interrupts your phone calls.	☐	☐
4. Five-year-old Bridget goes outside without asking your permission.	☐	☐
5. Nine-year-old Patrick doesn't finish his science project on time.	☐	☐
6. Thirteen-year-old Pam uses your ATM card without permission.	☐	☐

Now look back over your answers, and as a cross check, ask yourself who owns the problem (look back to chapter 5, if necessary). A good rule of thumb is that if the problem is the child's, then usually a natural consequence will occur and that will suffice. If the problem is yours, then there probably won't be a natural consequence, and you'll need to intervene with a logical consequence.

Answers:

1. It's possible that when Jillie throws sand at the other children at the playground, those children would retaliate—a natural consequence. It's also

possible that if you do nothing, another parent might intervene. However, since neither of these alternatives is inevitable, this situation requires a logical consequence. In addition, the health-and-safety factor of this behavior (in this case the health and safety of the other children) makes it your problem. If it's your problem, you need to apply a logical consequence.

2. Tom would experience the automatic natural consequences of not taking his raincoat if it were to rain. He would get wet and be very uncomfortable. Unless Tom has major health problems, getting wet would not present a serious risk. In this case, it's his problem. Let the natural consequence suffice. You don't need to do anything further.

3. There would be no automatic consequences to Rebeccah constantly interrupting your phone calls. It's your rights that are being infringed upon, and therefore this is your problem. You would need to apply a logical consequence.

4. It's uncertain whether anything would automatically happen to Bridget if she went outside without asking your permission—and it's exactly that uncertainty that you would want to avoid. Since Bridget's health and safety might be at risk from an unsupervised trip outside, this is your problem. Therefore you would need to apply a logical consequence. Of course, if you have an agreement with Bridget that she doesn't need your permission before going outside, then there is no problem.

5. Patrick would experience the automatic, natural consequences of not finishing his project. Therefore, you don't need to do anything further.

6. There would be no natural consequences to Pam's using your ATM card. This is your problem, and you would need to apply a logical consequence.

When to Use Consequences

Logical consequences can be used on their own or in conjunction with joint problem-solving strategies. When your angry three-year-old raises his arm to hit you, you might say, "Tell me in words or you'll have to go to your room for a time-out." There's no point in engaging in a lengthy problem-solving interaction at that moment. However, if the hitting continues despite the consequences, then in fact you might want to do some joint problem solving to determine how your son might be better encouraged to express himself verbally rather than physically.

In Step 6 of the problem-solving strategy (developing a plan for implementation and evaluation, and if possible a fallback plan), the fallback plan might be an appropriate logical consequence.

Consequences are also useful when a child is unwilling to participate in any problem-solving discussions.

Choices Before Consequences

Before applying a logical consequence, make sure a choice has been provided or at least implied. Present the alternatives, and then accept the child's choice, for instance: If you want me to wash your clothes, they need to be in the laundry hamper by Saturday at 10 a.m.; I'm trying to write a letter. You can either quiet down or go into the other room; You can have your bath either before dinner or after dinner. These are all examples of choices that you can provide.

There are three key guidelines to follow when designing logical consequences:

- Make sure the consequence is *related* to the misbehavior.
- Be prepared to *follow through* on the consequence.

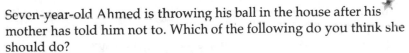

Present the consequence *without anger or blame*.

Make sure the consequence is related to the misbehavior. As mentioned before, in order to be effective a logical consequence must be logical. If the child can see the connection between his or her choices and the resulting consequences, the child will learn more easily to anticipate those consequences in the future—and therefore learn to make more responsible choices.

Related also means that the magnitude of the consequence needs to be consistent with the magnitude of the misbehavior. If there is a significant discrepancy between the two, the potential benefit to the child is greatly reduced, as the following stories illustrate.

✷ *Ahmed's Story* ✷

Seven-year-old Ahmed is throwing his ball in the house after his mother has told him not to. Which of the following do you think she should do?

A. Destroy the ball.

B. Send Ahmed to bed without any dinner.

C. Take away the ball for a certain, specified period of time.

D. Take away his bicycle for a certain, specified period of time.

Answer: Only alternative C is related in both content and magnitude. Therefore it is the only appropriate consequence. If Ahmed learns that when he misbehaves with his ball he doesn't get to play with his ball for a while, he may make different choices with the ball next time. The connection between misbehaving with his ball and getting no dinner or having his bike taken away would be much harder to understand and consequently harder to learn from. Having his ball destroyed would probably make Ahmed so angry that his learning would also be limited.

✶   *Sasha's Story*   ✶

Four-year-old Sasha is terribly excited about the camping trip that her family is packing for. In her enthusiasm, she dances around and generally gets underfoot. Her father has asked her several times to stay out of his way while he carries boxes to the car. Now he's getting really irritated. He growls at Sasha, "Either stay out of my way or . . ." How should he finish the sentence?

A. ". . . you're not coming with us."

B. ". . . you're going to have to stay in your bedroom while I finish packing."

C. ". . . you're not going to Ben's party next week."

Answer: Only alternative B is related both in content and magnitude, so it is the most appropriate consequence. The magnitude of alternative A far exceeds the misbehavior—even if her father were prepared to follow through on it (see the next paragraph)—while alternative C is unrelated to the misbehavior. Neither of these consequences would really teach Sasha about responsibility.

Be prepared to follow through on the consequence.

Once a consequence is established you have to follow through. If you say something is going to happen, then you must be prepared to make it happen or it will lose its ability to instruct. The flip side of this is to never set a consequence that you're not willing or able to follow through on. Otherwise you give your child the message that what you say isn't reliable. You undermine your own authority as well as the sense of consistency and stability that children need.

Present the consequence without anger or blame. The consequence that will follow from your child's choice must be presented neutrally. This way, you can remove yourself from the role of bad guy and avoid any fighting about the consequences. After all, the child made the choice, you are simply applying the consequences he or she has chosen, so no one is to blame. If you present the consequences with anger or gloatingly (I told you so), the lesson will again be lost in the child's anger and resentment. Anger turns a consequence into a punishment.

Time Out: Choice or Consequence?

Time out means just that: time away from whatever is going on. Usually this means that a child will go to his or her room for a specified amount of time. A few minutes is enough for a young child. This is not punishment. The child can go play with whatever toys he or she chooses in the room. Rather, this is a time for the child to reflect.

Time out can be useful in two ways. You can present it as one of two alternatives to your child, and let the decision be his or hers: "You can play quietly here, or you can go to your room and play more noisily." You can also present time out as a logical consequence of behaving inappropriately around others: "If you can't play nicely with your sister, then you'll have to go to your room." In both cases, the choice is essentially the child's.

Time out is particularly useful when the child's misbehavior occurs in a social setting. Time alone is an appropriate consequence for not choosing to behave appropriately around others.

Exercise: Choices and Consequences

For each of the examples below, first decide whether a natural consequence would automatically follow or a logical consequence would need to be applied. For the natural consequences, write an example of what the automatic consequence would be. For the logical consequences, write an example of the choices you might give the child, followed by the appropriate logical consequence.

	Natural	Logical
1. Despite your calling her, seven-year-old Carolyn is still in bed when you finish cooking breakfast.	☐	☐

_____

_____

_____

| 2. Six-year-old Bobby and his brother Alex fight loudly whenever you go anywhere in the car. | ☐ | ☐ |

_____

_____

_____

3. Three-year-old Allison crayons all over your
   freshly painted walls.   ☐   ☐

   _____

   _____

   _____

4. Five-year-old Morgan isn't dressed and the   ☐   ☐
   school bus is due in two minutes.

   _____

   _____

   _____

Answers:

1. If Carolyn is still in bed when breakfast is ready, there is no need for you to
   intervene. The natural consequence will be that she misses breakfast or that it
   will be cold by the time she comes for it.

2. When Bobby and Alex fight loudly in the car there won't be any natural
   consequences. The difficulty you experience concentrating on driving is your
   problem, and you will need to intervene with a logical consequence. That
   consequence might be that you have to stop driving until the noise stops, in
   which case you could pull off the road and read. Another might be that you
   turn around and go home, if driving becomes impossible, and Bobby and Alex
   therefore miss out on the excursion. In either case, you might express the

boys' choices to them in the following manner: "I can't drive with that noise. Either you quiet down or I'll have to . . ." pull off the road, go home, or whatever you decide.

3. When Allison scribbles on the walls, there won't be any natural consequences. You'll need to intervene with a logical consequence. If Allison has been tempted by the walls in the past, she might have already heard the choice: "Walls aren't for drawing on, only paper. If you draw on the walls, you're going to have to clean them." The logical consequence will require that you follow through with supervising while Allison cleaned up the wall (to the best of her ability).

4. If the school bus comes before Morgan is dressed, natural consequences will follow: She will either have to get on the bus without being properly dressed or she will miss the bus. These will occur without any intervention from you. If it's safe, she may have to walk to school. If not, you might drive her to school—when *you're* ready, without rushing—and her lateness will still incur natural consequences at school.

✴ *Carey and Janey* ✴

With all you've learned in this chapter, it is probably clear to you that Janey will need to apply a logical consequence to Carey's Easter egg extravaganza. If Janey follows the rules of separating the doer from the deed, avoiding punishment, and trying to make the consequence related to the misbehavior, she will need to eliminate the first seven of the options presented in the "Disciplining Carey" exercise and use the eighth option, or develop one of her own.

Learning how to provide appropriate choices and set appropriate limits is a challenge for all parents. If you don't always come up with the best choice or the perfect consequence, remember that you'll have plenty of other opportunities to do better. Your skills will improve with time and practice.

If you find yourself struggling with the temptation to punish because designing a consequence on the spur of the moment seems too difficult, tell your child that you need some time to think about how you want to respond and you will talk to him or her in a little while.

Keep in mind that your ultimate goal as a parent is to produce a mature, responsible adult. Simply asking yourself what you want your child to learn from this will help you remember to look for—and find—appropriate choices and consequences.

Keys to Designing Choices and Consequences

★   Present your child with choices that are valid and age appropriate.

★   Before you apply a consequence, a choice must be presented or implied.

★   Consequences may be natural (not requiring your intervention) or logical (requiring your intervention).

★   Logical consequences must be related to the misbehavior and presented without anger, and you must follow through on them.

★   Time out can be a choice or a consequence.

8

How to Choose Your Strategy

In the previous chapters you've learned many skills you can use in interacting with your child. You've learned about active listening and about expressing yourself. You've learned how to give choices and set consequences. And you've learned how to solve problems. How then do you decide which of those skills it is appropriate to use in any given situation?

Making that determination involves answering the question of whose problem it is (see chapter 5). The question of who owns the problem is directly related to the issue of whose rights are being violated. If your rights are being violated, it's your problem. If the other person's rights are being violated, it's his or her problem. Sometimes the distinction is clear, but at other times it's difficult to determine who owns the problem because both persons' rights are affected.

In this chapter you will learn to decide which skills to use, based on your understanding of who owns the problem.

When Your Child Owns the Problem

Your child might come to you with a problem involving a friend, a teacher, or simply himself or herself. A teacher could have yelled, a friend might have betrayed a secret, or a project could seem overwhelming. In these cases, there's no question that the child has a problem, and that your rights aren't involved.

To review, when the child owns the problem, the most effective skills are these:

★   Listen and validate your child's feelings (see chapter 3).

★   Encourage problem solving (see chapter 6).

It's important to remember that since the problem is not yours, it's not really up to you how (or whether) the problem gets solved. You may help or allow your child to come up with solutions that are right for him or her, but don't impose your own opinions.

When You Own the Problem

At other times you may see your child behaving in inappropriate ways that really do violate your rights. Your child might use your things without asking or damage something that belongs to you. He or she might call you names, scream at you, or otherwise behave disrespectfully. Similarly, your child might behave in ways that present a danger to himself or herself or to someone else.

It's clear that you own the problem under these circumstances—your child may not even be aware that there is a problem.

When you own the problem, it's your responsibility to take action. The most effective skills to use are these:

★ Express your feelings in an *I* statement (see chapter 4).

★ Engage your child in problem solving (see chapter 6).

★ If necessary, determine consequences (see chapter 7).

When the problem is not yours, it's not up to you how (or whether) the problem gets solved.

When You Both Have a Problem

Sometimes it's difficult to determine who owns the problem because both persons' rights are being affected. Your child may have a problem, but the way he or she tries to handle it creates a problem for you. Your child may sulk and be rude and disrespectful as a response to his or her problem.

When it's difficult to determine who owns the problem because both persons' rights are being affected, start with the child's problem. When that's resolved, your own problem may have been resolved in the process. The most effective skills to use are these:

★ Listen and validate your child's feelings (see chapter 3).

★ Encourage your child to solve his or her problem (see chapter 6).

If that doesn't resolve your problem, use these skills:

* Express your feelings in an *I* statement (see chapter 4).

* Engage your child in problem solving concerning your problem (see chapter 6).

* If necessary, determine consequences (see chapter 7).

This procedure is illustrated in the decision tree on page 122.

✳ *Curtis and Jesse's Story* ✳

Nine-year-old Jesse had had a hard time with his band teacher from day one. His father, Curtis, had talked with the teacher and with the parents of other kids in the band and had reached his own conclusion that the teacher was fine: Some people just rub each other the wrong way. Jesse wanted to complain about his teacher, but he didn't want to quit the band. It was hard for Curtis to listen to these complaints, especially since he believed them to be unfounded. His usual strategy was to defend the teacher.

One afternoon Jesse came home in a rage at the band teacher. "I hate him!" he stormed. "Just because we weren't perfect he said we can't perform in the all-schools night." Curtis knew how much Jesse had been looking forward to the performance—and how little he'd practiced. He was about to open his mouth to defend the teacher when he realized that this wasn't really his problem to solve. So he decided to try just listening and validating Jesse's experience. "Boy, that's really tough," he said, "especially since you were looking forward to it so much."

Jesse stopped pacing and sat down opposite Curtis at the kitchen table. "Yeah, I really was! You knew that. We all were. He was just looking for an excuse to drop us."

Next Curtis tried to encourage Jesse to do some problem solving. "What do you think you might do about it?" he asked. "I don't know," Jesse said gloomily. "I know what I feel like doing—but it'd land me in a lot more trouble than it's worth," he added with a dismal laugh. "Well, that's one possibility." replied Curtis, "Any others?"

"Well," admitted Jesse, "he did say that we'd have one more chance to show him what we can do on Thursday. I suppose if I practice really hard between now and then we might pull it off." He paused. Curtis held his tongue and waited. Jesse continued softly, "You know, we *were* sounding pretty awful. If I did my part better, we'd all sound better . . . I guess I haven't really practiced hard enough."

Working together, they came up with a practice plan for Jesse—an alternative that offered a lot more potential than Jesse following his impulse and acting out his anger at the teacher. Meanwhile, since Jesse was still somewhat skeptical of the band's chances, he reassured himself that they could try again next year if they didn't make it this year.

Curtis realized, accurately, that it wasn't his rights that were being violated in this situation. He reasoned that maybe it would help Jesse more for him to listen and validate his feelings, and then offer help in problem solving, than to get defensive on behalf of the teacher or to try and tell Jesse what to do to fix things. At the end of their time together, Jesse was feeling much less unhappy and less enraged. Curtis's assumptions and conclusions had been accurate.

Who Owns the Problem?

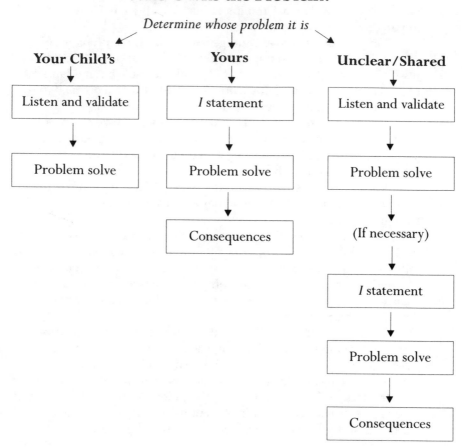

✳   *Maya and Starr's Story*   ✳

Maya's four-year-old daughter, Starr, had a habit of wandering into her mother's bedroom and playing with the articles on the bureau. Starr hadn't actually broken anything, but perfume had been spilled, Maya's ivory comb had temporarily been mislaid, and makeup had been smeared on the carpet as well as all over Starr's face. Maya had gotten angry at her daughter many times and told Starr that her behavior wasn't OK, but the problem didn't stop. And Maya was often too distracted with Starr's younger sister to keep track of what her older daughter was doing.

When you own the problem, it's your responsibility to take action.

Maya realized that this was her problem and her responsibility, and she decided to take a clearer stand. She expressed her feelings to her daughter in an *I* statement: "I get upset when you play with my stuff without asking. When I'm not here to supervise you, things get really messy, and I end up having to clean it up. And some things—like the carpet—I can't get clean. I would like you to not go into my bedroom unless I'm there with you. Do you understand?"

Starr hung her head and nodded. She seemed to understand, and for a week or so she stayed out of Maya's room. Then one afternoon, as Maya was putting her younger daughter down for a nap, she heard a crash from her bedroom. She rushed into the room. The scene was even worse than she had feared.

During the cleanup, Maya thought hard about what she should do next. She considered initiating some joint problem solving with Starr, but she decided that the situation called for a more authoritative response on her part. It was time for some consequences. There wasn't enough room in her cramped bedroom for Maya to find somewhere else to put the things that were at risk, so she pulled out her toolbox and installed a small hook-and-eye latch on her bedroom door, well above Starr's reach. Starr, watching her mother at work with the screwdriver, said tearfully, "I guess I should have asked. Now I can't ever go in." "Sure you can," replied Maya, "but only when you ask."

✦ *Emma and Angela's Story* ✦

According to her mother, Emma, six-year-old Angela had always been an easygoing child with a sunny personality. Then her baby brother, Leo, was born. Suddenly Angela felt that she'd been displaced in her parents' affection, or at least in their attention. She alternated between being loving and affectionate toward the new baby and being sullen and slyly aggressive. Most recently, Emma had caught Angela putting a pillow on the sleeping baby's face and tiptoeing away. All the patience and understanding with which Emma and her husband had been approaching Angela were rapidly disappearing.

Emma knew that Angela was having difficulties adjusting to her brother's arrival. And she realized that they were Angela's difficulties, not hers. However, Angela's aggressive behavior toward her baby brother *was* Emma's responsibility. She decided to try addressing Angela's problem first.

Angela wasn't saying much verbally about her feelings, so Emma "listened" to Angela's behavior. She said to Angela, "Sweetie, I know you love your brother. But I also know that it must be really hard at times to see your dad and me spending so much time and paying so much attention to him. I bet sometimes you wish we'd never had him." "No I don't!" retorted Angela defensively. There was a brief pause before she admitted, "Well, maybe sometimes."

Emma tried to validate those feelings, "You know, I hated my sister when she was born." "Auntie Sally?" asked Angela in disbelief. Emma nodded, "Yes, I once tried to throw her out the window! Hard to believe isn't it? It's lucky I was only three and couldn't unlatch the window." Angela, wide-eyed, said solemnly, "Wow. I don't think I *really* want something to happen to Leo. I just get so mad sometimes."

Emma decided to try encouraging some problem solving, "It's hard when those feelings are so strong. What do you think you could do at those times?" "Maybe I could come and talk to you about when you tried to throw Auntie Sally out the window?" suggested Angela. "That's a good idea. What else?" responded Emma. "I suppose I could go in my room and play," said Angela. "OK," said Emma, "Anything else?" "Well," teased Angela, "I could throw him down the garbage disposal!" "Or give him to Goodwill!" added Emma, laughing. "Just kidding," reassured Angela. Then they hugged.

Despite seeing an almost immediate change in Angela, Emma kept a close eye on her to ensure baby Leo's safety. On a few occasions, Angela did ask Emma to remind her about Auntie Sally. On another occasion she smiled at Emma and whispered, "I could flush him down the toilet!" To which Emma whispered back, "Or feed him to the raccoons!" But there were no more aggressive incidents, and

Angela seemed to be her old easygoing self. Emma realized that in helping Angela solve her problem, her own problem had been solved as well.

Exercise: Devising a Strategy

Using the decision tree shown on page 122, determine which of the strategies would be most effective in each of the following situations.

1. Your sweet-natured four-year-old has been unusually cranky recently and has reacted with a temper tantrum when asked to do certain things, such as clean up his toys, get ready for bed, or brush his teeth.

2. Your seven-year-old has started complaining that no one likes her at school and that she has no friends. She seems quite dejected.

3. Your two-year-old has developed a fascination for the toilet paper and keeps making her way into the bathroom and unrolling the entire roll.

Answers:

1. The first step is to determine who owns the problem. In this example, it seems clear, from his unusual behavior, that your four-year-old has a problem. At the same time, his behavior is creating a problem for you. Thus you both have a problem. The most effective response, therefore, would be to address your child's problem first:

    Listen and validate his feelings, first making sure you understand the problem by asking clarifying questions. Then encourage him in solving the problem.

If that doesn't resolve *your* problem, express your feelings in an *I* statement, and engage your son in problem solving. If nothing changes, then determine consequences.

2. In this example, your seven-year-old clearly owns the problem. Although it's disturbing to see someone you love in pain, it's important to remember that this is her problem and not yours. Under these circumstances, the most effective response would be to listen and validate her feelings and then encourage her in problem solving.

3. In this example, you definitely own the problem. Your two-year-old is having a wonderful time—she doesn't have a problem. Under these circumstances, the most effective response is to express your feelings in an *I* statement and determine consequences. Problem solving isn't a useful strategy with a two-year-old, and therefore it should be eliminated from the sequence in this situation.

At this point you have the basic skills necessary to deal with whatever problem situations arise for you—and your child. When you own the problem, it's your responsibility to take action and express yourself assertively. When your child owns the problem, the most useful response is to listen and validate. Encouraging problem solving may be useful, but it's important to remember that the other person may not be interested in solving the problem—and that's their choice because it's their problem. Only when your rights become involved does it become your problem and your responsibility.

Keys to Choosing Your Strategy

★ When your child owns the problem, listen and validate, and encourage problem solving.

★ When you own the problem, express your feelings in an *I* statement, engage your child in problem solving, and, if necessary, determine consequences.

★ When ownership of the problem is unclear because both persons' rights are affected, listen and validate the child's feelings and encourage the child to solve his or her problem. If that doesn't solve *your* problem, express your feelings in an *I* statement, engage your child in solving your problem, and if necessary, determine consequences.

9

How to Cope with Anger

Parenting is the hardest job in the world, with long unpaid hours of noisy, messy, repetitive, exhausting, frustrating work. Anyone might occasionally develop feelings of anger when working under such conditions. It would be hard even if parents could focus solely on their job as parents. With all the other competing responsibilities in their lives, anger becomes inevitable.

Studies indicate that many parents are concerned—for good reason—about how frequently and how intensely they express anger toward their children. Of particular concern is corporal (physical) punishment. It's a very small step from excessive anger to abuse, and the growing epidemic of child abuse in this country is frightening.

Even nonabusive anger isn't helpful—especially to children. As you learned in chapter 7, on choices and consequences, anger is frightening and causes children to feel unsafe. They begin to believe that they must be terribly bad people to deserve such treatment. And anger begets more anger. Children who have been exposed to a lot of anger are more likely to express their own anger in aggressive ways than others not exposed to such conditions.

This chapter will help you learn how to cope more effectively with your angry feelings by using such strategies as combating your trigger thoughts, reducing the stress in your life, asking for what you want, and planning ahead.

Why You Get Angry

When you're really stressed, getting angry can actually make you feel better. It can discharge or relieve tension caused by other painful feelings (emotional or physical) or unmet needs or desires. Alternatively, it can also serve to block awareness of such uncomfortable feelings. When you're anxious you feel vulnerable and helpless, whereas when you're angry you feel much more powerful. Therefore feeling angry can seem easier—or at least preferable—to feeling anxious, scared, guilty, or ashamed.

★   *Amelia and John's Story*   ★

Amelia was waiting for her ten-year-old son, John, to get home from soccer practice. It was already five o'clock, and he should have been home half an hour ago. As the minutes ticked by, Angela's anxiety grew. She could no longer concentrate on what she was doing.

Instead her mind was filled with images of John amid the mangled remains of his bicycle.

At 5:15 she heard the front door open, and John sauntered into the kitchen. Realizing that John was unhurt—and therefore had no excuse for worrying her so much—Amelia's anxiety was immediately discharged by an angry outburst. Her feelings of relief were so fleeting she barely registered them.

John, who had had a flat tire on his bike and was feeling tremendously proud of himself for having changed it by himself, was crushed by his mother's rage. It was a blow not only to his self-esteem, but also to their relationship.

✳ *Janet and Anthony's Story*   ✳

Four-year-old Anthony knew that his mother, Janet, was hurt. She'd been in a car accident. For two weeks after her release from the hospital, she had had to stay in bed. Anthony's grandmother had come to live with them and take care of Janet and, of course, him. What Anthony didn't know was that, although his mother was now able to walk around a little with the use of crutches, she was still in some pain and tired easily. Anthony also didn't know how much his mother worried about him, felt guilty for burdening her own mother, and fretted about getting back to her job. She was also pretty fed up with her condition.

Anthony got up from his afternoon quiet time and went bouncing in to see his mother. "Hi, Mommy-wommy!" he called as—without thinking—he launched himself onto the bed.

Janet winced and bit her lip. "Be careful!" she said roughly.

"Play with me?" Anthony coaxed. "Not right now," Janet responded. "Please, please, just for five minutes?" Anthony wheedled. "Just go away and leave me alone!" Janet exploded, turning her face to the wall. Anthony, lips quivering, eyes filling with tears, left the room.

Janet's anger not only discharged the tension that had built from her anxiety and frustration, it also temporarily distracted her from her physical pain. Unfortunately, her outburst of anger was traumatic for Anthony and threatened—over time—the security of their relationship. It's not difficult to see that although anger might make you feel temporarily better, the long-term effects on any relationship can be devastating.

Exercise: Understanding Anger

Think about the last time you got angry with someone. Briefly describe the situation leading up to the anger.

_____

_____

_____

_____

Now, using the assumption that anger serves a purpose by either discharging or blocking awareness of other painful feelings (emotional or physical) or frustrated needs or desires, try to identify the underlying stress. Were you feeling anxious, scared, depressed, hurt, disappointed, guilty, or ashamed? Were you experiencing physical pain, muscle tension, overstimulation, or fatigue? Were needs or desires being frustrated? If so, what were they?

_____

_____

_____

_____

How You Get Angry   *assigning motivation*

What enables the rapid transition from one feeling (anxiety, frustration, disappointment, pain) to another (anger)? Anger has two essential requirements: stress and trigger thoughts.

Trigger thoughts are those that ignite stressful feelings into anger. They usually take one of the following forms:

- They ascribe negative traits to the misbehaving person—"You're so lazy/stubborn/selfish/cruel."

- They assume a negative intent behind his or her behavior—"You're doing this deliberately to hurt me."

- Or they magnify the behavior to intolerable proportions—"I can't stand this, this is unbearable."

Stress by itself is not enough to cause an angry outburst. Without trigger thoughts you simply have stressful feelings. Trigger thoughts allow you to shift responsibility for those painful feelings to someone else—and then to justify your anger toward that person.

For example, if your daughter says she's going to clean up her room and doesn't, you'll probably feel disappointed and maybe a little frustrated—not really angry. But if at the same time you think to yourself "I can't believe she lied to me again. She's so selfish," you'll notice a rapid transition into anger and outrage.

Another example: If your child throws a temper tantrum in public, your first reaction is probably going to be embarrassment and frustration. Not anger. But combine those stressful feelings with the thought "He's deliberately trying to humiliate me in public. I won't tolerate this!" and once again you'll experience a rapid escalation into anger and outrage.

Stress by itself is not enough to cause an angry outburst.

✶ Amelia and John ✶

Amelia had been profoundly anxious about John's safety when he hadn't arrived home at the expected time. Had she been willing to endure the anxiety, she probably could have experienced her relief in his safety more fully and gone on to express some of both her relief and her anxiety to John. Together they might have come to some kind of resolution that enhanced their relationship.

Instead, Amelia triggered anger and outrage with the thoughts, "He's so damn selfish and thoughtless. He knows I sit here and worry, and he can't be bothered getting here on time. And then to saunter in as if everything was OK—it drives me crazy." With such thoughts, Amelia could justify her rage at John rather than having to endure her anxiety.

⭐ *Janet and Anthony* ⭐

After weeks of slow, painful recovery from her accident, Janet felt frustrated by her persistent weakness and fatigue, anxious about her job, guilty about the burden on her own mother, and in pain. If she'd been willing to endure those stressful feelings, she could have talked about them with her mother, and maybe even a little with Anthony. With their help, she might have been able to develop a plan for addressing some of her emotional and physical pain.

Instead, Janet triggered a hostile, angry outburst with the thoughts, "Why can't you be more careful? I can't stand it! Just get off my back." With such thoughts she could justify her unprovoked anger at her son rather than having to take responsibility for addressing her pain.

Exercise: Identifying Trigger Thoughts

Look back at the preceding exercise, in which you identified a situation where you were angry and then identified the underlying stressful feelings or frustrated needs or desires. This time try to identify what was going through your head as you were beginning to experience that underlying stress. What were you thinking? Did you ascribe negative traits to the person involved? Did you assume there was a negative intention behind his or her behavior? Did you magnify the seriousness of the actions? Write down these trigger thoughts.

_____

_____

Coping with Anger

First recognizing and then changing your trigger thoughts is an essential part of coping with anger. The following are nine ways to reduce anger. The first four deal specifically with changing your trigger thoughts. The rest have to do with changing the way you act and react.

Develop coping statements.   Come up with, and memorize, some brief messages that can help you keep your cool in stressful situations. For example:

- ★   Relax, stay calm.

- ★   I'm staying calm. I don't have to get angry to cope with this.

- ★   He/she is doing the best he/she can right now. He/she is not trying to upset me.

- ★   I may not like what's happening, but I can cope with it without anger.

Remembered and silently repeated whenever you feel yourself beginning to get angry, these coping statements will calm you and help you look for more constructive choices than anger.

Assess the real cause.   Parents often assume that their children misbehave deliberately to provoke them—to punish them, to test them, to drive them crazy, to "get at" them. Researchers and child development specialists find that this is rarely the case. Torturing their parents is not often a motive for children.

It's important to look at other factors to discover the real cause of your child's behavior. As discussed in chapter 1, one such factor is temperament—the built-in wiring that each child is issued at or before birth—the way he or she tends to respond to life experiences. Characteristics that determine temperament include general activity level, basic disposition, ability to adapt to change, distractibility, and persistence. It doesn't make sense to get angry with a child whose shyness, high activity level, or difficulty with transitions is temperamental.

Another important consideration is that the main task of childhood is to gain independence and autonomy. In order to achieve this goal, a child has to learn to make decisions and choices, experience the consequences of those decisions and choices, and develop a sense of separateness from his or her parents. That means that much of a child's behavior is aimed—appropriately—at demonstrating his or her separateness: testing the limits, disobeying parental rules, and trying to control the outcome of different situations. Again, it doesn't help to get angry with a child who's doing what children are supposed to do.

Finally, when assessing the real cause of the behavior, it's important to remember that children's behavior is primarily an attempt to meet their needs. These needs can range from the more fundamental (to achieve significance, to feel autonomous, to belong) to the more everyday (to get praise, attention, physical nurturing, sleep, food, or help doing something or solving a problem). If you can try to understand and meet those needs, it may lead to a change in the behavior. At the very least, the attempt may distract you from your anger.

Replace negative labels. To reduce your anger, you must avoid those provocative terms that make you see red, such as *lazy, spoiled, thoughtless, cruel,* and *stupid.* Replacing these labels with a clear, accurate, *neutral* description of what's happening is hard to do, but it really works. It means sticking to just the facts, as if you were an investigator. When your son doesn't provide you with the information you requested about the school fundraiser, you could simply label him as selfish and lazy—and chances are you'd rapidly escalate into anger. Instead, ask yourself what exactly is happening here. Then answer with just the facts: "I asked Andrew to provide me with the information today, and he didn't. I don't know why." If you don't have all the facts, ask your child for his or her input. The process will go very differently. Without labels, your anger will be far easier to control.

Assess the magnitude of the problem. How truly serious is the problem? Avoid thinking such things as "It's outrageous," "Completely intolerable," "Totally ridiculous," "I can't believe that . . ." Replace these provocative exaggerations with accurate, behavioral descriptions of exactly what's happening: "Andrew didn't provide me with the information today, and I need it to calculate projected sales for the school. I wish he'd brought it, but since the fundraiser is still a week away, I can probably manage if I get the necessary data in the next day or so." The absence of trigger thoughts prevents an escalation into anger.

Use a time-out. To prevent the situation from escalating and to think about an appropriate response, take a break. Review chapter 7 on choices and consequences so that you can be clear about what you want from your child and about the consequences of his or her noncompliance. A few minutes apart will give you time to calm down and think about your desired response. Giving the child a time-out—a few minutes in his or her room—can sometimes be a sufficient consequence by itself. Or you can take the time-out yourself. Leave the situation for a few minutes: Go to the bathroom and wash your face. Get yourself a tall glass of water and drink it. Make a cup of tea. Take a deep breath and count to fifty—very slowly.

Practice relaxation. The more stress in your life in general, the easier it is to be provoked into anger. The early signs of anger include increased muscle tension (clenched jaw or fists, a constricted feeling in the chest, butterflies in the stomach), and a shift in breathing pattern (heavy or rapid breathing, feeling short of breath). Breathing deeply requires that your chest and belly expand, and enables the slow, full replenishing of oxygen to the lungs, so it is almost impossible to breathe deeply and maintain a high level of stress.

Deep breathing exercises provide an antidote to stress and therefore a valuable tool in the fight against anger. To practice deep breathing use the following steps:

1. Sit or lie down in a relaxed position and put one hand on your belly.

2. Inhale slowly and deeply, pushing the air down into your belly and making the hand resting there rise.

3. Gently exhale with a slow whooshing sound, keeping your muscles relaxed and saying to yourself "Relax."

4. Continue to take long, slow, deep breaths into your belly and let them out gently. Focus on the sound and movement of your belly and notice how you become more and more relaxed.

The more frequently you practice this breathing exercise, the more impact it will have in your life. A few minutes a day will counteract some of the ups and downs of daily life. And a concentrated effort to use it before responding to a provocative situation will enable you to avoid escalating into anger.

Identify what you need and ask for it. As discussed above, there are often feelings underlying your anger: disappointment, guilt, shame, embarrassment. Once you can identify the feeling, ask yourself what you need to do to take care of it. If you're feeling embarrassed about your child having a tantrum in the supermarket, perhaps you need to remind yourself that you're a good parent. If you're feeling guilty about your two-year-old hitting another child in the playground, perhaps you need to remind yourself that this is a stage that he or she will outgrow with adequate guidance from you and as he or she develops the necessary language skills.

Once you've identified what you need, ask for it assertively (review chapter 4 on expressing yourself, if necessary). When you see your four-year-old jumping up and down on the new couch, it may take some effort to refrain from screaming at him. But you'll be more successful in the long run if—after lifting him off—you can say something assertive, such as, "I get really nervous when I see you jumping on the new couch. That couch just cost me a lot of money, and I don't want it broken or damaged—or you to get hurt either. You can either sit on it nicely, or go to your room."

Get support.   Parenting is a tough business. It's important that you get all the support you can. Read the next chapter, on taking care of yourself, to explore how to do this.

Plan ahead.   In some cases, if you can anticipate situations that have the potential for triggering anger, you can devise a coping strategy. This reduces the chances of being caught off guard and reacting explosively. The following exercise walks you through the planning process. The steps in planning to head off anger use the strategies discussed above.

Note: You may want to make photocopies of these pages to use for different behaviors that make you angry.

Exercise: Heading Off Anger

Think about the ways your child typically behaves that make you angry.

Pick one example of your child's behavior that regularly makes you angry.

_____

_____

_____

Identify your typical trigger thoughts related to that behavior.

_____

_____

_____

Develop some coping statements to say to yourself when it occurs next time.

_____

_____

_____

Think of possible explanations for the behavior other than those negative attributions described in your trigger thoughts.

Temperament:

_____

_____

_____

Could this be age-appropriate behavior?

_____

_____

_____

What needs could your child be trying to meet?

_____

_____

_____

Plan an assertive statement to ask for what you want or need, and determine what choices and consequences you will set, if appropriate.

Assertive statement:

_____

_____

_____

Choices and consequences (if appropriate):

_____

_____

_____

Repeat this process for all the problem behaviors you identified.

A Note on Your Child's Anger

Anger is inevitable at some times for everyone. As you've learned in earlier chapters, there's nothing wrong with your child having angry feelings. However, the way your child chooses to express those feelings may be inappropriate, and might require you to set limits about what is and is not OK behavior. This is no different from setting limits on any other behavior that you deem inappropriate—that is any time the problem is yours.

On the other hand, if your child seems to express a lot of anger a lot of the time, you can help your child learn modified versions of the strategies described to cope more effectively with his or her anger. Identifying and changing trigger thoughts, assessing the real cause and magnitude of the problem behavior, learning some relaxation or breathing techniques, asking assertively for what is wanted, and planning ahead are all things that children can incorporate to varying degrees. You will need to adapt the strategies to the child's age and abilities.

Anger is one of the hardest emotions to cope with appropriately. It probably feels at times like you have no control over your anger at all. Yet you live in an age where access to lethal weapons is terrifyingly easy, and giving in to anger can have violent, devastating consequences. Starting with your own small part of the world and taking responsibility for your own anger, you can help decrease the anger and potential violence in the world as a whole. The strategies discussed in this chapter can help you make a significant start in that direction.

Keys to Coping with Anger

★ Develop coping statements to replace trigger thoughts.

★ Assess the real cause of your child's behavior.

★ Replace negative labels with neutral descriptions.

★ Realistically assess the magnitude of the problem.

★ Use a time-out to prevent escalation.

★ Practice relaxation through deep breathing.

★ Identify what you want and ask for it assertively.

★ Plan ahead.

★ Get support.

How to Take Care of Yourself

As you read in chapter 1, the need for nurturing doesn't cease just because you have grown up. As an adult you need nurturing just as much as ever, in part because life becomes more complex and burdensome than it was (or should have been) as a child. However, the responsibility for nurturing now rests on your own shoulders.

It's remarkably easy—with the pressure of parenting responsibilities, or employment—to let self-nurturing activities drop to the bottom of the priority list. But it's a mistake to think of nurturing yourself as an indulgence. Not only is it essential to your well-being as a parent, but it teaches your children that others' needs are important, and that being a parent doesn't mean you have to stop taking care of yourself.

Parenting is one of the hardest jobs in the world. The hours are long and filled with repetitious, boring, dirty, and often frustrating tasks, with few tangible, short-term rewards. Even worse, our society doesn't fully value child care nor see it as the investment in the future of the world that it truly is. Thus parents receive little outside recognition for the vital work that they do.

This chapter will help you develop ways of nurturing yourself as a person as well as as a parent.

Why Is Self-Care So Important for Parents?

Before you become a parent, the division between work and play is fairly clear. With some exceptions, you work during the week and then play and rest on the weekends. Even if you love your job, there's little question that having time to play is essential to your well-being.

When you become a parent, that division suddenly becomes fuzzier. You still work all day, either at a job outside the house or at the job of parenting, but at five o'clock the job doesn't stop and you don't get to go home and play—or rest. Nor does it stop on weekends. The job of parenting can stretch into every spare minute of the day and well into the night. And you don't get a paycheck for those extra hours.

To keep up to the job, it's important that you take care of yourself on a regular basis. You wouldn't expect your car to perform satisfactorily if you didn't regularly fill the gas tank and change the oil. Nor should you expect any different of yourself.

The following are ways you might nurture yourself on a regular basis. The more of these that you incorporate into your life, the more energy and fullness you'll have to pass on to your children. Keep in mind that the activities described below are just a few of the many possible ways you might nurture yourself.

Take time for yourself.   Rest, read, have a bubble bath, listen to music, or do whatever else that feels nurturing to you. Carve out an hour for yourself while the baby naps in the afternoon or after he or she goes to bed at night. Ignore the dishes sitting in the sink or the clothes that need washing just for that hour. Remind yourself that nurturing yourself is at least as important as housework.

What are some activities that you find nurturing?

_____

_____

_____

_____

_____

_____

_____

Share your thoughts and feelings.   On a regular basis, make time to talk with a friend or your partner about what you think and feel, about your frustrations and dilemmas.

There are many frustrations in being a parent, and one of the most frustrating aspects is that you rarely get to talk to other adults while you're on the job. If you make time on a regular basis to talk to someone you trust, you'll be less likely to store up your frustrations and then take them out on your child or partner.

Who do you currently talk to regularly or who might you be able to talk to?

_____   _____

_____   _____

_____   _____

Do something fun. It's often fun to do things with your child. But it's important to remember that you had a life before you had a child and will have one after he or she leaves home, so it will help to have maintained some interests throughout. Try to find something to do that's challenging or interesting, and also fun: attend a class, take up a sport, join a quilting bee and make a quilt. In order to do this, get a babysitter if you can afford one, even for a couple of hours. Or ask a friend or family member to watch the child for a while. Check your community resources. Some agencies (such as Parental Stress) have drop-in child care for periods of up to a couple of hours—enough time to fill your metaphorical gas tank. Look in the yellow pages under Social Services Organizations for information on drop-in child care.

Treat yourself. Once in a while, give yourself something special: get a manicure or a facial, have a massage, take yourself out to lunch at a nice restaurant, go for a walk on the beach or to a movie in the afternoon. As a conscientious parent, your focus is more likely to be on reinforcing your child for good behavior than on rewarding yourself. It's important every now and then to change that focus.

Eat well. Taking care of yourself physically is the foundation of feeling well emotionally. When you're hungry and your blood sugar is low, you're likely to be more irritable, have a lower threshold for frustration, and be less able to solve problems effectively. Most parents are conscientious about ensuring that their children eat a healthy, balanced diet, but they are all too willing to skip a meal themselves. It's not healthy for you, nor is it good modeling for your child.

Get some exercise. Exercise not only keeps you physically healthy, but it can reduce stress and even depression. Find something that works for you: Put your child in the stroller and head around the block. Run up and down the stairs a dozen times. Get an exercise video and let your child work out with you.

Get enough sleep. Once again, this is about taking care of yourself physically. Everyone knows that when you're well rested you can more easily handle frustration and solve problems. Unfortunately, with babies, sleep deprivation is part of the package. As children get older, it's easy for parents to fall into the trap of trying to survive with just as little sleep—after all, there's so much to do and so little time.

Decide what's essential, and let the rest go.

Let some things go. Life is all about making choices—so is parenting. Sometimes the decisions are about what to do. Sometimes they're about what *not* to do, what to let go. This makes perfect sense. If your life is full before you have a child, then adding the work of raising a child means there isn't going to be time for everything else. Something has to go, at least some of the time.

Maybe you take particular pride in your appearance and spend hours in front of the mirror, or maybe you like to keep your car in mint condition—waxed and polished and gleaming. Perhaps you strive for perfection in every job or assignment you undertake. Maintaining those same expectations once a child arrives on the scene will increase your stress and probably lead to feelings of failure. Decide what's essential, and let the rest go.

Spend time alone with your partner. If you have a partner in parenting, it will probably be a lot easier to accomplish some of these self-nurturing suggestions than if you're a single parent. As partners, you can occasionally relieve each other, if even for a few minutes. However, don't forget that it's important to nurture your couple relationship. You and your partner need time for the two of you to maintain your bond. The couple relationship is the foundation for your parenting relationship, and keeping a compatible partnership will benefit your children.

Get support. If you're a single parent, getting support is essential. The task of parenting is much harder when you're alone. Friends and family can be extremely important resources. Don't be embarrassed about asking for help—and the more specific you can be, the better. Ask your sister to bring you an occasional home-cooked meal so you don't have to worry about dinner that night. Ask your mother to watch the baby for an evening. Ask your best friend to come and keep you company during the worst hours with your colicky baby.

Nurturing yourself is an essential part of being a good parent. Juggling all the responsibilities of nurturing a child, working at a job, maintaining a relationship, and helping run a household are all hard work, and it's easy to forget that it's your responsibility to keep a balance between work and play in your life.

Parenting may be the hardest work of all, but it can also be one of the most rewarding. Taking care of yourself enables you to maintain the strength not only to cope with the endless hours and worries, but also to reap the rewards.

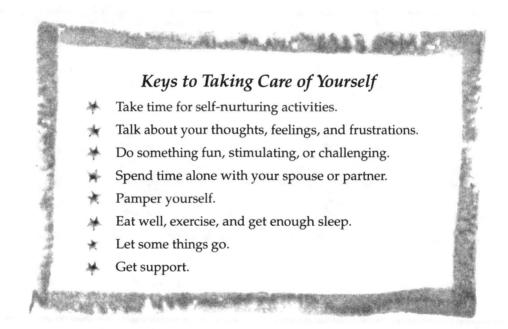

Keys to Taking Care of Yourself

- Take time for self-nurturing activities.
- Talk about your thoughts, feelings, and frustrations.
- Do something fun, stimulating, or challenging.
- Spend time alone with your spouse or partner.
- Pamper yourself.
- Eat well, exercise, and get enough sleep.
- Let some things go.
- Get support.

Epilogue

Now that you've reached the end of this book and have mastered the ten key concepts, you should be ready to handle almost anything.

However, it's important to remember that child-rearing is inherently a process of trial and error. Since every child is different, what works for one won't necessarily work for another—or even for the same child at a different age. You have to use the concepts in different ways until you find something that works for your child at the time.

For simplicity of presentation in this book, the ten concepts are handled discreetly. Unfortunately, real life is never so straightforward. While keeping in mind the key concepts, remember that they will have to be combined when you are dealing with different situations. For example, you can't help your child solve a problem without combining at least the three concepts of listening, determining who owns the problem, and problem solving.

So good luck—and enjoy yourself!

References

Kahn, Michael. 1991. *Between Therapist and Client: The New Relationship.* New York: W. H. Freeman.

McKay, Matthew, Patrick Fanning, Kim Paleg, and Dana Landis. 1996. *When Anger Hurts Your Kids.* Oakland, California: New Harbinger Publications.

Smith, Manuel J. 1975. *When I Say No I Feel Guilty.* New York: Bantam Books.

Turecki, Stanley, and Leslie Tonner. 1985. *The Difficult Child.* New York: Bantam Books.